Pastoral Care of the Sick

PASTORAL CARE OF THE SICK

CUIDADO PASTORAL DE LOS ENFERMOS

Liturgy Training Publications

Mexican American Cultural Center

ACKNOWLEDGMENTS

Concordat cum originali: Reverend John A. Gurrieri, Executive Director
Bishops' Committee on the Liturgy, National
Conference of Catholic Bishops

Published by authority of the Bishops' Committee on the Liturgy, National Conference of Catholic Bishops

English translation prepared by the International Commission on English in the Liturgy, taken from the *Ordo Unctionis infirmorum eorumque pastoralis curae,* Editio Typica, Typis Polyglottis Vaticanis, 1972. The translation has been approved by the National Conference of Catholic Bishops, 18 November 1982. Confirmed by Decree of the Sacred Congregation for the Sacraments and Divine Worship, Protocol CD 1207/82, 11 December 1982.

Additional copies of this book may be obtained from:

Liturgy Training Publications
1800 North Hermitage Avenue
Chicago IL 60622–1101
312/486–7008

Mexican American Cultural Center
3019 West French Place
San Antonio TX 78228
512/732–2156

ISBN 0–930467–54–X

FOREWORD

Peace and joy in the Lord to you, Minister to the sick and to the aged and infirm. We are happy to see that this bilingual edition of *Pastoral Care of the Sick* is in your hands and we hope that you will find it helpful in your ministry. This book is an abridged edition which in no way replaces the complete editions available in English or in Spanish. This edition is intended simply to be a practical help to both those who speak Spanish fluently and those who do not.

The numbers of chapters and paragraphs found in this book correspond to those in the complete versions. The numbers here are therefore not continuous.

We have included decrees from the United States bishops and the Sacred Congregation for Divine Worship, as well as the Apostolic Constitution on the Sacrament of the Anointing of the Sick and the introductions to the parts and chapters as found in the complete editions. These are valuable instruments that will help you to understand and to appreciate the beautiful ministry to which you have been called. Read these carefully and reflect on them.

All the rites are given in English and Spanish. The English text on the left side will always correspond exactly to the Spanish on the right side. This should facilitate use by those ministers who are not fluent in both languages. We are aware of the great number of Spanish-speaking Catholics who come to our hospitals and nursing homes, and of so many others who remain invalids at home. In their moments of suffering, you will bring great consolation by celebrating with them the rites of the sick in their own language.

The editors and all of us who have been involved in any way in this project would like to acknowledge the work done by Rick Flores in the beginning stages of this book and by Sister Rosa María Icaza, CCVI, in the later stages. We are grateful to them.

May God continue to bless your efforts, Minister to the sick, as you bring consolation and peace to the sick and the dying.

+ Ricardo Ramírez, CSB
Bishop of Las Cruces, New Mexico

CONTENTS

DECREE

NATIONAL CONFERENCE OF CATHOLIC BISHOPS
UNITED STATES OF AMERICA

In accord with the norms established by decree of the Sacred Congregation of Rites *Cum, nostra aetate* (27 January 1966), *Pastoral Care of the Sick: Rites of Anointing and Viaticum* is declared to be the vernacular *editio typica* of the *Ordo Unctionis infirmorum eorumque pastoralis curae* for the dioceses of the United States of America, and may be published by authority of the National Conference of Catholic Bishops.

Pastoral Care of the Sick: Rites of Anointing and Viaticum was canonically approved by the National Conference of Catholic Bishops in plenary assembly on 18 November 1982 and was subsequently confirmed by the Apostolic See by decree of the Sacred Congregation for the Sacraments and Divine Worship on 11 December 1982 (Prot. CD 1207/82).

On 1 September 1983 *Pastoral Care of the Sick: Rites of Anointing and Viaticum* may be published and used in celebrations for the sick and dying. The mandatory effective date has been established by the conference of bishops as 27 November 1983, the First Sunday of Advent. From that day forward no other vernacular versions of these rites may be used.

Given at the General Secretariat of the National Conference of Catholic Bishops, Washington, D.C., on 28 January 1983, the Memorial of Saint Thomas Aquinas, priest and doctor.

+ John R. Roach
Archbishop of Saint Paul and Minneapolis
President
National Conference of Catholic Bishops

Daniel F. Hoye
General Secretary

DECREE

SACRED CONGREGATION FOR DIVINE WORSHIP

Prot. no. 1501/72

When the Church cares for the sick, it serves Christ himself in the suffering members of his Mystical Body. When it follows the example of the Lord Jesus, who "went about doing good and healing all" (Acts 10:38), the Church obeys his command to care for the sick (see Mark 16:18).

The Church shows this solicitude not only by visiting those who are in poor health but also by raising them up through the sacrament of anointing and by nourishing them with the eucharist during their illness and when they are in danger of death. Finally, the Church offers prayers for the sick to commend them to God, especially in the last crisis of life.

To make the meaning of the sacrament of anointing clearer and more evident, Vatican Council II decreed: "The number of the anointings is to be adapted to the circumstances; the prayers that belong to the rite of anointing are to be so revised that they correspond to the varying conditions of the sick who receive the sacrament."[1] The Council also directed that a continuous rite be prepared according to which the sick person is anointed after the sacrament of penance and before receiving viaticum.[2]

In the Apostolic Constitution *Sacram Unctionem infirmorum* of 30 November 1972, Pope Paul VI established a new sacramental form of anointing and approved the *Ordo Unctionis infirmorum eorumque pastoralis curae.* The Congregation for Divine Worship prepared this rite and now issues it, declaring this to be the *editio typica* so that it may replace the pertinent sections that are now in the Roman Ritual.

Anything to the contrary notwithstanding.

From the ofice of the Congregation for Divine Worship, 7 December 1972.

Arturo Cardinal Tabera
Prefect

+ Annibale Bugnini
Titular Archbishop of Diocletiana
Secretary

---

[1] Vatican Council II, Constitution on the Liturgy, art. 75: *Acta Apostolicae Sedis* (AAS) 56 (1964) 119.

[2] See ibid., art. 74: AAS 119.

2

APOSTOLIC CONSTITUTION
SACRAMENT OF THE ANOINTING
OF THE SICK

PAUL, BISHOP
Servant of the Servants of God
For an Everlasting Memorial

The Catholic Church professes and teaches that the anointing of the sick is one of the seven sacraments of the New Testament, that it was instituted by Christ our Lord, "intimated in Mark (6:13) and through James, the apostle and brother of the Lord, recommended to the faithful and made known: 'Is there anyone sick among you? Let him send for the presbyters of the Church and let them pray over him, anointing him with oil in the name of the Lord. The prayer of faith will save the sick man and the Lord will raise him up. If he has committed any sins, they will be forgiven him' (James 5:14-15)."[1]

From ancient times there is evidence of the anointing of the sick in the Church's tradition, particularly in the liturgical tradition, both in the East and in the West. Worthy of special note are the letter which Innocent I, our predecessor, addressed to Decentius, Bishop of Gubbio,[2] and also the ancient prayer used for blessing the oil of the sick, "Lord, . . . send the Holy Spirit, our Helper and Friend. . . ." This prayer was inserted in the eucharistic prayer[3] and is still preserved in the Roman Pontifical.[4]

In the course of centuries of liturgical tradition, the parts of the body to be anointed with holy oil were more explicitly defined in different ways. Several formularies of prayer were added to accompany the anointings and these are contained in the liturgical books of various Churches. In the Church of Rome during the Middle Ages the custom prevailed of anointing the sick on the senses with the formulary: *Per istam sanctam Unctionem, et suam piissimam misericordiam, indulgeat tibi Dominus quidquid deliquisti*, with the name of each sense added.[5]

In addition, the teaching concerning the sacrament of anointing is expounded in the documents of the ecumenical Councils of Florence, Trent especially, and Vatican II.

After the Council of Florence had described the essential elements of the sacrament of the anointing of the sick,[6] the Council of Trent declared that it was of divine institution and explained what is taught in the Letter of James concerning holy anointing, especially about the reality signified and the effects of the sacrament: "This reality is in fact the grace of the Holy Spirit, whose anointing takes away sins, if any still remain, and the remnants of sin; this anointing also raises up and strengthens the soul of the sick person, arousing a great confidence in the divine mercy; thus sustained, the sick person may more easily bear the trials and hardships of sickness, more easily resist the temptations of the devil 'lying in wait for his heel' (Genesis 3:15), and sometimes regain bodily health, if this is expedient for the health of the soul."[7] The same Council also declared that these words of the apostle state with sufficient clarity that "this anointing is to be given to the sick, especially those who are in such a serious condition as to appear to have reached the end of their life. For this reason it is also called the sacrament of the dying."[8] Finally, the Council declared that the presbyter is the proper minister of the sacrament.[9]

Vatican Council II adds the following: "'Extreme unction,' which may also and more properly be called 'anointing of the sick,' is not a sacrament for those only who are at the point of death. Hence, as soon as any one of the faithful begins to be in danger of death from sickness or old age, the fitting time for that person to receive this sacrament has certainly already arrived."[10] The use of this sacrament is a concern of the whole Church: "By the sacred anointing of the sick and the prayer of its presbyters, the whole Church commends the sick to the suffering and glorified Lord so that he may raise them up and save them (see James 5:14-16). The Church exhorts them, moreover, to contribute to the welfare of the whole people of God by associating themselves willingly with the passion and death of Christ (see Romans 8:17; Colossians 1:24; 2 Timothy 2:11-12; 1 Peter 4:13)."[11]

All these considerations had to be weighed in revising the rite of anointing in order better to adapt to present-day conditions those elements which were subject to change.[12]

We have thought fit to modify the sacramental form in such a way that, by reflecting the words of James, it may better express the effects of the sacrament.

Since olive oil, which has been prescribed until now for the valid celebration of the sacrament, is unobtainable or difficult to obtain in some parts of the world, we have decreed, at the request of a number of bishops, that from now on, according to circumstances, another kind of oil can also be used, provided it is derived from plants, and is thus similar to olive oil.

As regards the number of anointings and the parts of the body to be anointed, it has seemed opportune to simplify the rite.

Therefore, since this revision in certain points touches upon the sacramental rite itself, by our apostolic authority we establish that the following is to be observed for the future in the Latin rite:

THE SACRAMENT OF THE ANOINTING OF THE SICK IS GIVEN TO THOSE WHO ARE SERIOUSLY ILL BY ANOINTING THEM ON THE FOREHEAD AND HANDS WITH BLESSED OLIVE OIL OR, ACCORDING TO CIRCUMSTANCES, WITH ANOTHER BLESSED PLANT OIL AND SAYING ONCE ONLY THESE WORDS:

4

THROUGH THIS HOLY ANOINTING
MAY THE LORD IN HIS LOVE AND MERCY HELP YOU
WITH THE GRACE OF THE HOLY SPIRIT.

MAY THE LORD WHO FREES YOU FROM SIN
SAVE YOU AND RAISE YOU UP. *

In case of necessity, however, it is sufficient that a single anointing be given on the forehead or, because of the particular condition of the sick person, on another suitable part of the body, while the whole sacramental form is said.

The sacrament may be repeated if the sick person recovers after being anointed and then again falls ill or if during the same illness the person's condition becomes more serious.

Having made these decisions and declarations about the essential rite of the sacrament of the anointing of the sick, by our apostolic authority we also approve the *Ordo Unctionis infirmorum eorumque pastoralis curae*, which has been revised by the Congregation for Divine Worship. At the same time, where necessary we amend the prescriptions of the Code of Canon Law or other laws hitherto in force or we repeal them; other prescriptions and laws, which are neither repealed nor amended by the above-mentioned rite, remain valid and in force. The Latin edition containing the new rite will come into force as soon as it is published; the vernacular editions, prepared by the conferences of bishops and confirmed by the Apostolic See, will come into force on the dates to be laid down by the individual conferences. The old rite may be used until 31 December 1973. From 1 January 1974, however, only the new rite is to be used by those concerned.

We intend that everything we have laid down and prescribed should be firm and effective in the Latin rite, notwithstanding, where relevant, the apostolic constitutions and ordinances issued by our predecessors and other prescriptions, even if worthy of special mention.

Given at Rome, at Saint Peter's, 30 November 1972, the tenth year of our pontificate.

Paul VI

---

*LATIN: Per istam sanctam unctionem et suam piissimam misericordiam, adiuvet te Dominus gratia Spiritus Sancti, ut a peccatis liberatum te salvet atque propitius allevet.

[1] Council of Trent, sess. 14, De Extrema Unctione, cap. 1 (see also can. 1): *Concilium Tridentinum* (CT), vol. 7, pt. 1, 355-356; Denz.-Schön. 1695, 1716.

[2] See Innocent I, Ep. *Si Instituta Ecclesiastica*, cap. 8: PL 20, 559-561; Denz.-Schön. 216.

[3] See L.C. Mohlberg, ed., *Liber Sacramentorum Romanae Aeclesiae Ordinis Anni Circuli* in *Rerum Ecclesiasticarum Documenta, Fontes* 4 (Rome, 1960) 61; J. Deshusses, ed., *Le Sacramentaire Grégorien*, in *Spicilegium Friburgense* 16 (Fribourg, 1971) 172. See also B. Botte, ed., *La Tradition Apostolique de Saint Hippolyte* in *Liturgiewissenschaftliche Quellen und Forschungen* 39 (Münster-W., 1963) 18-19; E. Lanne, ed., *Le Grand Euchologie du Monastère Blanc* in *Patrologia Orientalis* 28, pt. 2 (Paris, 1958) 392-395.

[4] See Roman Pontifical, *Rite of Blessing of Oils, Rite of Consecrating the Chrism*, no. 20 [*The Sacramentary* (*The Roman Missal*) Appendix II].

[5] See M. Andrieu, *Le Pontifical Romain au Moyen-Age*, vol. 1, *Le Pontifical Romain du XIIe siècle* in *Studi e Testi* 86 (Vatican City, 1938) 267-268; vol. 2, *Le Pontifical de la Curie Romaine au XIIIe siècle* in *Studi e Testi* 87 (Vatican City, 1940) 491-492.

[6] See Council of Florence, *Decr. pro Armeniis*: G. Hofmann, *Concilium Florentinum*, vol. 1, pt. 2 (Rome, 1944) 130; Denz.-Schön. 1324-1325.

[7] Council of Trent, sess. 14, De Extrema Unctione, cap. 2: CT 7, 1, 356; Denz.-Schön. 1696.

[8] Ibid., cap. 3: CT, ibid.; Denz.-Schön. 1698.

[9] See ibid., cap. 3, can. 4: CT, ibid.; Denz.-Schön. 1697, 1719.

[10] Vatican Council II, Constitution on the Liturgy, art. 73: AAS 56 (1964) 118-119.

[11] Vatican Council II, Dogmatic Constitution on the Church, no. 11: AAS 57 (1965) 15.

[12] See Vatican Council II, Constitution on the Liturgy, art. 1: AAS 56 (1964) 97.

PASTORAL CARE OF THE SICK
Rites of Anointing and Viaticum

GENERAL INTRODUCTION

HUMAN SICKNESS AND ITS MEANING IN THE MYSTERY OF SALVATION

1   Suffering and illness have always been among the greatest problems that trouble the human spirit. Christians feel and experience pain as do all other people; yet their faith helps them to grasp more deeply the mystery of suffering and to bear their pain with greater courage. From Christ's words they know that sickness has meaning and value for their own salvation and for the salvation of the world. They also know that Christ, who during his life often visited and healed the sick, loves them in their illness.

2   Although closely linked with the human condition, sickness cannot as a general rule be regarded as a punishment inflicted on each individual for personal sins (see John 9:3). Christ himself, who is without sin, in fulfilling the words of Isaiah took on all the wounds of his passion and shared in all human pain (see Isaiah 53:4-5). Christ is still pained and tormented in his members, made like him. Still, our afflictions seem but momentary and slight when compared to the greatness of the eternal glory for which they prepare us (see 2 Corinthians 4:17).

3   Part of the plan laid out by God's providence is that we should fight strenuously against all sickness and carefully seek the blessings of good health, so that we may fulfill our role in human society and in the Church. Yet we should always be prepared to fill up what is lacking in Christ's sufferings for the salvation of the world as we look forward to creation's being set free in the glory of the children of God (see Colossians 1:24; Romans 8:19-21).

Moreover, the role of the sick in the Church is to be a reminder to others of the essential or higher things. By their witness the sick show that our mortal life must be redeemed through the mystery of Christ's death and resurrection.

4   The sick person is not the only one who should fight against illness. Doctors and all who are devoted in any way to caring for the sick should consider it their duty to use all the means which in their judgment may help the sick, both physically and spiritually. In so doing, they are fulfilling the command of Christ to visit the sick, for Christ implied that those who visit the sick should be concerned for the whole person and offer both physical relief and spiritual comfort.

CELEBRATION OF THE SACRAMENTS
FOR THE SICK AND THE DYING

ANOINTING OF THE SICK

5   The Lord himself showed great concern for the bodily and spiritual welfare of the sick and commanded his followers to do likewise. This is clear from the gospels, and above all from the existence of the sacrament of anointing, which he instituted and which is made known in the Letter of James. Since then the Church has never ceased to celebrate this sacrament for its members by the anointing and the prayer of its priests, commending those who are ill to the suffering and glorified Lord, that he may raise them up and save them (see James 5:14-16). Moreover, the Church exhorts them to associate themselves willingly with the passion and death of Christ (see Romans 8:17),[1] and thus contribute to the welfare of the people of God.[2]

Those who are seriously ill need the special help of God's grace in this time of anxiety, lest they be broken in spirit and, under the pressure of temptation, perhaps weakened in their faith.

This is why, through the sacrament of anointing, Christ strengthens the faithful who are afflicted by illness, providing them with the strongest means of support.[3]

The celebration of this sacrament consists especially in the laying on of hands by the priests of the Church, the offering of the prayer of faith, and the anointing of the sick with oil made holy by God's blessing. This rite signifies the grace of the sacrament and confers it.

6   This sacrament gives the grace of the Holy Spirit to those who are sick: by this grace the whole person is helped and saved, sustained by trust in God, and strengthened against the temptations of the Evil One and against anxiety over death. Thus the sick person is able not only to bear suffering bravely, but also to fight against it. A return to physical health may follow the reception of this sacrament if it will be beneficial to the sick person's salvation. If necessary, the sacrament also provides the sick person with the forgiveness of sins and the completion of Christian penance.[4]

7   In the anointing of the sick, which includes the prayer of faith (see James 5:15), faith itself is manifested. Above all this faith must be made actual both in the minister of the sacrament and, even more importantly, in the recipient. The sick person will be saved by personal faith and the faith of the Church, which looks back to the death and resurrection of Christ, the source of the sacrament's power (see James 5:15),[5] and looks ahead to the future kingdom that is pledged in the sacraments.

RECIPIENTS OF THE ANOINTING OF THE SICK

8   The Letter of James states that the sick are to be anointed in order to raise them up and save them.[6] Great care and concern should be taken to see that those of the faithful whose health is seriously* impaired by sickness or old age receive this sacrament.[7]

A prudent or reasonably sure judgment, without scruple, is sufficient for deciding on the seriousness of an illness;[8] if necessary a doctor may be consulted.

9   The sacrament may be repeated if the sick person recovers after being anointed and then again falls ill or if during the same illness the person's condition becomes more serious.

10   A sick person may be anointed before surgery whenever a serious illness is the reason for the surgery.

11   Elderly people may be anointed if they have become notably weakened even though no serious illness is present.

12   Sick children may be anointed if they have sufficient use of reason to be strengthened by this sacrament. In a case of doubt whether a child has reached the use of reason, the sacrament is to be conferred.[8 bis]

13   In public and private catechesis, the faithful should be educated to ask for the sacrament of anointing and, as soon as the right time comes, to receive it with full faith and devotion. They should not follow the wrongful practice of delaying the reception of the sacrament. All who care for the sick should be taught the meaning and purpose of the sacrament.

14   The sacrament of anointing is to be conferred on sick people who, although they have lost consciousness or the use of reason, would, as Christian believers, have at least implicitly asked for it were they in control of their faculties.[9]

15   When a priest has been called to attend those who are already dead, he should not administer the sacrament of anointing. Instead, he should pray for them, asking that God forgive their sins and graciously receive them into the kingdom. But if the priest is doubtful whether the sick person is dead, he is to confer the sacrament, using the rite given in no. 269.[10]

The anointing of the sick is not to be conferred on anyone who remains obdurately in open and serious sin.

---

*The word *periculose* has been carefully studied and rendered as "seriously," rather than as "gravely," "dangerously," or "perilously." Such a rendering will serve to avoid restrictions upon the celebration of the sacrament. On the one hand, the sacrament may and should be given to anyone whose health is seriously impaired; on the other hand, it may not be given indiscriminately or to any person whose health is not seriously impaired.

MINISTER OF THE ANOINTING OF THE SICK

16   The priest is the only proper minister of the anointing of the sick.[11]
This office is ordinarily exercised by bishops, pastors and their assistants, chaplains of health-care facilities, and superiors of clerical religious institutes.[12]

17   These ministers have the pastoral responsibility both of preparing and helping the sick and others who are present, with the assistance of religious and laity, and of celebrating the sacrament.
The diocesan bishop has the responsibility of supervising celebrations at which sick persons may come together to receive the sacrament.

18   For a reasonable cause any other priest may confer this sacrament with at least the presumed consent of the minister mentioned in no. 16, whom the priest need only inform later.

19   When two or more priests are present for the anointing of a sick person, one of them may say the prayers and carry out the anointings, saying the sacramental form. The others may take the remaining parts, such as the introductory rites, readings, invocations, or instructions. Each priest may lay hands on the sick person.

REQUIREMENTS FOR CELEBRATING THE ANOINTING OF THE SICK

20   The matter proper for the sacrament is olive oil or, according to circumstances, other oil derived from plants.[13]

21   The oil used for anointing the sick must be blessed for this purpose by the bishop or by a priest who has this faculty, either from the law or by special concession of the Apostolic See.
The law itself permits the following, besides a bishop, to bless the oil of the sick:
   a) those whom the law equates with diocesan bishops;
   b) in case of necessity, any priest, but only within the celebration of the sacrament.[14]

The oil of the sick is ordinarily blessed by the bishop on Holy Thursday.[15]

22   If a priest, in accord with no. 21 b, is to bless the oil during the rite, he may bring the unblessed oil with him, or the family of the sick person may prepare the oil in a suitable vessel. If any of the oil is left after the celebration of the sacrament, it should be absorbed in cotton and burned.
If the priest uses oil that has already been blessed (either by the bishop or by a priest), he brings it with him in the vessel in which it is kept. This vessel, made of suitable material, should be clean and should contain sufficient oil

(soaked in cotton for convenience). In this case, after celebrating the sacrament the priest returns the vessel to the place where it is kept with proper respect. He should make sure that the oil remains fit for use and should replenish it from time to time, either yearly when the bishop blesses the oil on Holy Thursday or more frequently if necessary.

23   The sick person is anointed on the forehead and on the hands. It is appropriate to divide the sacramental form so that the first part is said while the forehead is anointed, the latter part while the hands are anointed.

In case of necessity, however, it is sufficient that a single anointing be given on the forehead or, because of the particular condition of the sick person, on another suitable part of the body, while the whole sacramental form is said.

24   Depending on the culture and traditions of different peoples, the number of anointings may be increased and the place of anointing may be changed. Directives on this should be included in the preparation of particular rituals.

25   The following is the sacramental form with which the anointing of the sick is given in the Latin rite:

> Through this holy anointing
> may the Lord in his love and mercy help you
> with the grace of the Holy Spirit.
>
> May the Lord who frees you from sin
> save you and raise you up.

VIATICUM FOR THE DYING

26   When in their passage from this life Christians are strengthened by the body and blood of Christ in viaticum, they have the pledge of the resurrection that the Lord promised: "Those who eat my flesh and drink my blood have eternal life, and I will raise them up on the last day" (John 6:54).

When possible, viaticum should be received within Mass so that the sick person may receive communion under both kinds. Communion received as viaticum should be considered a special sign of participation in the mystery which is celebrated in the eucharist: the mystery of the death of the Lord and his passage to the Father. [16]

27   All baptized Christians who are able to receive communion are bound to receive viaticum by reason of the precept to receive communion when in danger of death from any cause. Priests with pastoral responsibility must see that the celebration of this sacrament is not delayed, but that the faithful are nourished by it while still in full possession of their faculties. [17]

28   It is also desirable that during the celebration of viaticum, Christians renew the faith professed at their baptism, by which they became adopted children of God and coheirs of the promise of eternal life.

29   The ordinary ministers of viaticum are the pastor and his assistants, chaplains, and, for all staying in the house, the superior in clerical religious institutes or societies of apostolic life.

In case of necessity or with at least the presumed permission of the competent minister, any priest or deacon is to give viaticum, or, if no ordained minister is available, any member of the faithful who has been duly appointed.

A deacon and other ministers follow the rite provided for "Viaticum outside Mass," nos. 197–211.

CONTINUOUS RITE

30   For special cases, when sudden illness or some other cause has unexpectedly placed one of the faithful in proximate danger of death, a continuous rite is provided by which the sick person may be given the sacraments of penance, anointing, and the eucharist as viaticum in a single celebration.

If death is imminent and there is not enough time to celebrate the three sacraments in the manner already described, the sick person should be given an opportunity to make a sacramental confession, even if it has to be a generic confession. After this the person should be given viaticum, since all the faithful are bound to receive this sacrament if they are in danger of death. Then, if there is sufficient time, the sick person should be anointed.

The sick person who, because of the nature of the illness, cannot receive communion should be anointed.

31   If the person is to be strengthened by the sacrament of confirmation, nos. 238, 246, 276, 290, and 291 of this ritual should be consulted.

In danger of death, the law gives the faculty to confirm to pastors and in fact to any priest.[18]

OFFICES AND MINISTRIES FOR THE SICK

32   If one member suffers in the Body of Christ, which is the Church, all the members suffer with that member (1 Corinthians 12:26).[19] For this reason, kindness shown toward the sick and works of charity and mutual help for the relief of every kind of human want are held in special honor.[20] Every scientific effort to prolong life[21] and every act of care for the sick, on the part of any person, may be considered a preparation for the Gospel and a sharing in Christ's healing ministry.[22]

33   It is thus especially fitting that all baptized Christians share in this ministry of mutual charity within the Body of Christ by doing all that they can to help the sick return to health, by showing love for the sick, and by celebrating the sacraments with them. Like the other sacraments, these too have a community aspect, which should be brought out as much as possible when they are celebrated.

34   The family and friends of the sick and those who take care of them in any way have a special share in this ministry of comfort. In particular, it is their task to strengthen the sick with words of faith and by praying with them, to commend them to the suffering and glorified Lord, and to encourage them to contribute to the well-being of the people of God by associating themselves willingly with Christ's passion and death.[23] If the sickness grows worse, the family and friends of the sick and those who take care of them have the responsibility of informing the pastor and by their kind words of prudently disposing the sick for the reception of the sacraments at the proper time.

35   Priests, particularly pastors and the others mentioned in no. 16, should remember that it is their duty to care for the sick by personal visits and other acts of kindness.[24] Especially when they give the sacraments, priests should stir up the hope of those present and strengthen their faith in Christ who suffered and is glorified. By bringing the Church's love and the consolation of faith, they comfort believers and raise the minds of others to God.

36   It is important that all the faithful, and above all the sick, be aided by suitable catechesis in preparing for and participating in the sacraments of anointing and viaticum, especially if the celebration is to be carried out communally. In this way they will understand more fully what has been said about the anointing of the sick and about viaticum, and the celebration of these sacraments will nourish, strengthen, and manifest faith more effectively. For the prayer of faith which accompanies the celebration of the sacrament is nourished by the profession of this faith.

37   When the priest prepares for the celebration of the sacraments, he should ask about the condition of the sick person. He should take this information into account, for example, in planning the rite, in choosing readings and prayers, and in deciding whether he will celebrate Mass when viaticum is to be given. As far as possible, he should arrange all this with the sick person and the family beforehand, when he explains the meaning of the sacraments.

ADAPTATIONS BELONGING TO
THE CONFERENCES OF BISHOPS

38   In virtue of the Constitution on the Liturgy (art. 63 b), the conferences of bishops have the right to prepare a section in particular rituals corresponding to the present section of the Roman Ritual and adapted to the needs of the different parts of the world. This section is for use in the regions concerned once the *acta* have been reviewed by the Apostolic See.

The following are the responsibilities of the conferences of bishops in this regard:

a) to decide on the adaptations dealt with in the Constitution on the Liturgy, article 39;

b) to weigh carefully and prudently what elements from the traditions and culture of individual peoples may be appropriately admitted into divine worship, then to propose to the Apostolic See adaptations considered useful or necessary that will be introduced with its consent;

c) to retain elements in the rites of the sick that now exist in particular rituals, as long as they are compatible with the Constitution on the Liturgy and with contemporary needs; or to adapt any of these elements;

d) to prepare translations of the texts so that they are truly adapted to the genius of different languages and cultures and to add, whenever appropriate, suitable melodies for singing;

e) to adapt and enlarge, if necessary, this Introduction in the Roman Ritual in order to encourage the conscious and active participation of the faithful;

f) to arrange the material in the editions of liturgical books prepared under the direction of the conferences of bishops in a format that will be as suitable as possible for pastoral use.

39   Whenever the Roman Ritual gives several alternative texts, particular rituals may add other texts of the same kind.

ADAPTATIONS BY THE MINISTER

40 The minister should take into account the particular circumstances, needs, and desires of the sick and of other members of the faithful and should willingly use the various opportunities that the rites provide.

a) The minister should be especially aware that the sick tire easily and that their physical condition may change from day to day and even from hour to hour. For this reason the celebration may be shortened if necessary.

b) When there is no group of the faithful present, the priest should remember that the Church is already present in his own person and in the one who is ill. For this reason he should try to offer the sick person the love and help of the Christian community both before and after the celebration of the sacrament. He may ask another Christian from the local community to do this if the sick person will accept this help.

c) Sick persons who regain their health after being anointed should be encouraged to give thanks for the favor received by participating in a Mass of thanksgiving or by some other suitable means.

41 The priest should follow the structure of the rite in the celebration, while accommodating it to the place and the people involved. The penitential rite may be part of the introductory rite or take place after the reading from Scripture. In place of the thanksgiving over the oil, the priest may give an instruction. This alternative should be considered when the sick person is in a hospital and other sick people present do not take part in the celebration of the sacrament.

---

[1] See also Colossians 1:24; 2 Timothy 2:11-12; 1 Peter 4:13.

[2] See Council of Trent, sess. 14, De Extrema Unctione, cap, 1: Denz.-Schön. 1695; Vatican Council II, Dogmatic Constitution on the Church, no. 11: AAS 57 (1965) 15.

[3] See Council of Trent, sess. 14, De Extrema Unctione, cap. 1: Denz.-Schön. 1694.

[4] See ibid., prooem. and cap. 2: Denz.-Schön. 1694 and 1696.

[5] See St. Thomas Aquinas, In 4 Sententiarum, d. 1, q. 1, a. 4, quaestiuncula 3.

[6] See Council of Trent, sess. 14, De Extrema Unctione, cap. 2: Denz.-Schön. 1698.

[7] See Vatican Council II, Constitution on the Liturgy, art. 73: AAS 56 (1964) 118-119.

[8] See Pius XI, Epist. Explorata res, 2 February 1923: AAS 15 (1923) 103-107.

[8 bis] See CIC, can. 1005.

[9] See CIC, can. 1006.

[10] See CIC, can. 1005.

[11] See Council of Trent, sess. 14, De Extrema Unctione, cap. 3 and can. 4: Denz.-Schön. 1697 and 1719; CIC, can. 1003, § 1.

[12] See CIC, can. 1003, § 2.

[13] See Roman Pontifical, *Rite of Blessing of Oils, Rite of Consecrating the Chrism*, Introduction, no. 3 [*The Sacramentary* (*The Roman Missal*) Appendix II].

[14] See CIC, can. 999.

[15] See Roman Pontifical, *Rite of Blessing of Oils, Rite of Consecrating the Chrism*, Introduction, no. 9.

[16] See Congregation of Rites, Instruction *Eucharisticum mysterium*, 25 May 1967, nos. 36, 39, 41: AAS 59 (1967) 561, 562, 563.

[17] See Congregation of Rites, Instruction *Eucharisticum mysterium*, 25 May 1967, no. 39: AAS 59 (1967) 562.

[18] See, *Rite of Confirmation*, Introduction, no. 7c.

[19] See Vatican Council II, Dogmatic Constitution on the Church, no. 7: AAS 57 (1965) 9-10.

[20] See Vatican Council II, Decree on the Apostolate of the Laity, no. 8: AAS 58 (1966) 845.

[21] See Vatican Council II, Pastoral Constitution on the Church in the Modern World, no. 18: AAS 58 (1966) 1038.

[22] See Vatican Council II, Dogmatic Constitution on the Church, no. 28: AAS 57 (1965) 34.

[23] See ibid., no. 21: AAS 57 (1965) 24.

[24] See CIC, can. 529, § 1.

PART I

PASTORAL CARE OF THE SICK

Part I
PASTORAL CARE OF THE SICK

INTRODUCTION

Lord, your friend is sick.

42   The rites in Part I of *Pastoral Care of the Sick: Rites of Anointing and Viaticum* are used by the Church to comfort the sick in time of anxiety, to encourage them to fight against illness, and perhaps to restore them to health. These rites are distinct from those in the second part of this book, which are provided to comfort and strengthen a Christian in the passage from this life.

43   The concern that Christ showed for the bodily and spiritual welfare of those who are ill is continued by the Church in its ministry to the sick. This ministry is the common responsibility of all Christians, who should visit the sick, remember them in prayer, and celebrate the sacraments with them. The family and friends of the sick, doctors and others who care for them, and priests with pastoral responsibilities have a particular share in this ministry of comfort. Through words of encouragement and faith they can help the sick to unite themselves with the sufferings of Christ for the good of God's people.

    Remembrance of the sick is especially appropriate at common worship on the Lord's Day, during the general intercessions at Mass and in the intercessions at Morning Prayer and Evening Prayer. Family members and those who are dedicated to the care of the sick should be remembered on these occasions as well.

44   Priests have the special task of preparing the sick to celebrate the sacrament of penance (individually or in a communal celebration), to receive the eucharist frequently if their condition permits, and to celebrate the sacrament of anointing at the appropriate time. During this preparation it will be especially helpful if the sick person, the priest, and the family become accustomed to praying together. The priest should provide leadership to those who assist him in the care of the sick, especially deacons and other ministers of the eucharist.

    The words "priest," "deacon," and "minister" are used advisedly. Only in those rites which must be celebrated by a priest is the word "priest" used in the rubrics (that is, the sacrament of penance, the sacrament of the anointing of the sick, the celebration of viaticum within Mass). Whenever it is clear that, in the absence of a priest, a deacon may preside at a particular rite, the words "priest or deacon" are used in the rubrics. Whenever another minister is permitted to celebrate a rite in the absence of a priest or deacon, the word "minister" is used in the rubrics, even though in many cases the rite will be celebrated by a priest or deacon.

45   The pastoral care of the sick should be suited to the nature and length of the illness. An illness of short duration in which the full recovery of health is a possibility requires a more intensive ministry, whereas illness of a longer duration which may be a prelude to death requires a more extensive ministry. An awareness of the attitudes and emotional states which these different situations engender in the sick is indispensable to the development of an appropriate ministry.

VISITS TO THE SICK

46   Those who visit the sick should help them to pray, sharing with them the word of God proclaimed in the assembly from which their sickness has separated them. As the occasion permits, prayer drawn from the psalms or from other prayers or litanies may be added to the word of God. Care should be taken to prepare for a future visit during which the sick will receive the eucharist.

VISITS TO A SICK CHILD

47.   What has already been said about visiting the sick and praying with them (see no. 46) applies also in visits to a sick child. Every effort should be made to know the child and to accommodate the care in keeping with the age and comprehension of the child. In these circumstances the minister should also be particularly concerned to help the child's family.

48.   If it is appropriate, the priest may discuss with the parents the possibility of preparing and celebrating with the child the sacraments of initiation (baptism, confirmation, eucharist). The priest may baptize and confirm the child (see *Rite of Confirmation*, no. 7b). To complete the process of initiation, the child should also receive first communion. (If the child is a proper subject for confirmation, then he or she may receive first communion in accordance with the practice of the Church.) There is no reason to delay this, especially if the illness is likely to be a long one.

49   Throughout the illness the minister should ensure that the child receives communion frequently, making whatever adaptations seem necessary in the rite for communion of the sick (Chapter Three).

50   The child is to be anointed if he or she has sufficient use of reason to be strengthened by the sacrament of anointing. The rites provided (Chapter Four) are to be used and adapted.

COMMUNION OF THE SICK

51   Because the sick are prevented from celebrating the eucharist with the rest of the community, the most important visits are those during which they receive holy communion. In receiving the body and blood of Christ, the sick are united sacramentally to the Lord and are reunited with the eucharistic community from which illness has separated them.

ANOINTING OF THE SICK

52   The priest should be especially concerned for those whose health has been seriously impaired by illness or old age. He will offer them a new sign of hope: the laying on of hands and the anointing of the sick accompanied by the prayer of faith (James 5:14). Those who receive this sacrament in the faith of the Church will find it a true sign of comfort and support in time of trial. It will work to overcome the sickness, if this is God's will.

53   Some types of mental sickness are now classified as serious. Those who are judged to have a serious mental illness and who would be strengthened by the sacrament may be anointed (see no. 5). The anointing may be repeated in accordance with the conditions for other kinds of serious illness (see no. 9).

Chapter One

VISITS TO THE SICK

Chapter One

VISITS TO THE SICK

INTRODUCTION

I was sick, and you visited me.

54   The prayers contained in this chapter follow the common pattern of reading, response, prayer, and blessing. This pattern is provided as an example of what can be done and may be adapted as necessary. The minister may wish to invite those present to prepare for the reading from Scripture, perhaps by a brief introduction or through a moment of silence. The laying on of hands may be added by the priest, if appropriate, after the blessing is given.

55   The sick should be encouraged to pray when they are alone or with their families, friends, or those who care for them. Their prayer should be drawn primarily from Scripture. The sick person and others may help to plan the celebration, for example, by choosing the prayers and readings. Those making these choices should keep in mind the condition of the sick person.

The scripture passage found in this chapter speaks of the mystery of human suffering. Occasionally, for example, on the Lord's Day, the sick may feel more involved in the worship of the community from which they are separated if the readings used are those assigned for that day in the lectionary. Prayers may also be drawn from the psalms or from other prayers or litanies. The sick should be helped in making this form of prayer, and the minister should always be ready to pray with them.

56   The minister should encourage the sick person to offer his or her sufferings in union with Christ and to join in prayer for the Church and the world. Some examples of particular intentions which may be suggested to the sick person are: for peace in the world; for a deepening of the life of the Spirit in the local Church; for the pope and the bishops; for people suffering in a particular disaster.

23

VISITS TO THE SICK

OUTLINE OF THE RITE
Reading
Response
Lord's Prayer
Concluding Prayer
Blessing

VISITAS A LOS ENFERMOS

ESQUEMA DEL RITO
    Lectura
    Respuesta a la Palabra
    Padrenuestro
    Oración conclusiva
    Bendición

VISITS TO THE SICK

READING

57   The word of God is proclaimed by one of those present or by the minister.

A reading from the Acts of the Apostles   3:1-10

In the name of Jesus and the power of his Church, there is salvation — even liberation from sickness.

Once, when Peter and John were going up to the Temple for the prayers at the ninth hour, it happened that there was a man being carried past. He was a cripple from birth; and they used to put him down every day near the Temple entrance called the Beautiful Gate so that he could beg from the people going in.

When this man saw Peter and John on their way into the Temple he begged from them. Both Peter and John looked straight at him and said, "Look at us."

He turned to them expectantly, hoping to get something from them, but Peter said, "I have neither silver nor gold, but I will give you what I have: in the name of Jesus Christ the Nazarene, walk!" Peter then took him by the hand and helped him to stand up.

Instantly his feet and ankles became firm, he jumped up, stood, and began to walk, and he went with them into the Temple, walking and jumping and praising God.

Everyone could see him walking and praising God, and they recognized him as the man who used to sit begging at the Beautiful Gate of the Temple. They were all astonished and unable to explain what had happened to him.

This is the Word of the Lord.

VISITAS A LOS ENFERMOS

LECTURA

57.   Uno de los presentes o un ministro proclama la palabra de Dio.

Lectura del libro de los Hechos de los Apóstoles   3,1-10

En el nombre de Jesús y con el poder de su Iglesia hay salvación, más aún, liberación de la enfermedad.

Pedro y Juan subían al Templo para la oración de las tres de la tarde. Había allí un hombre tullido de nacimiento, al que llevaban y ponían todos los días junto a la puerta del Templo, llamada "Puerta Hermosa", para que pidiera limosna a los que entraban.

El inválido, al ver que Pedro y Juan entraban en el Templo, les pidió limosna. Pedro, con Juan a su lado, se fijó en él y le dijo: "Míranos".

El tullido los miró fijamente, esperando recibir algo. Pedro entonces le dijo: "No tengo oro ni plata, pero lo que tengo, te lo doy: en nombre de Jesús de Nazaret, camina". Y lo tomó de la mano derecha y lo levantó.

Inmediatamente sus tobillos y sus pies recuperaron la fuerza, y de un salto se puso de pie y caminó. Entró con ellos en el Templo andando, saltando y alabando a Dios.

Todo el pueblo lo vio caminar y alabar a Dios. Lo reconocían como el tullido que pedía limosna junto a la Puerta Hermosa del Templo y quedaron asombrados y maravillados por lo que había sucedido.

Esta es palabra de Dios.

RESPONSE

58.   A brief period of silence may be observed after the reading of the word of God. The following psalm may be used:

Psalm 102

R.   O Lord, hear my prayer and let my cry come to you.

O Lord, listen to my prayer
and let my cry for help reach you.
Do not hide your face from me
in the day of my distress.
Turn your ear towards me
and answer me quickly when I call.

R.   O Lord, hear my prayer and let my cry come to you.

He has broken my strength in mid-course;
He has shortened the days of my life.
I say to God: "Do not take me away
before my days are complete,
you, whose days last from age to age."

R.   O Lord, hear my prayer and let my cry come to you.

Let this be written for ages to come
that a people yet unborn may praise the Lord;
for the Lord leaned down from his sanctuary on high.
He looked down from heaven to the earth
that he might hear the groans of the prisoners
and free those condemned to die.

R.   O Lord, hear my prayer and let my cry come to you.

The minister may then give a brief explanation of the reading, applying it to the needs of the sick person and those who are looking after him or her.

LORD'S PRAYER

59.   The minister introduces the Lord's Prayer in these or similar words:

Now let us offer together the prayer our Lord Jesus Christ taught us:

All say:

Our Father . . .

RESPUESTA A LA PALABRA

58. Se puede guardar silencio después de la lectura de la palabra de Dios. Enseguida se puede utilizar el salmo siguiente:

Salmo 102

R.   Señor, escucha mi plegaria;
que a tu presencia lleguen mis clamores.

Señor, escucha mi plegaria
y que mi clamor llegue a tu presencia.
No apartes tu rostro de mí;
en el tiempo de mi angustia préstame atención;
escúchame en el día que te invoco. R.

El ha consumido mis fuerzas
en el camino y ha acortado mi vida.
Pero yo digo: Dios mío,
no cortes mi vida en la mitad del camino,
tú que eres eterno. R.

Se habrá de escribir para los tiempos futuros,
y un pueblo nuevo alabará al Señor.
Porque miró desde su glorioso templo,
y se inclinó del cielo hacia la tierra.
Para oír el gemido de los cautivos,
y librar a los condenados a muerte. R.

El ministro puede a continuación hacer una breve explicación de la lectura, tratando de aplicarla a las necesidades de la persona enferma y de aquellos (aquellas) que la cuidan.

PADRENUESTRO

59.   El ministro introduce el padrenuestro con estas o semejantes palabras:

Oremos confiadamente al Padre con las palabras que nos enseñó nuestro Salvador:

Todos dicen:

Padre nuestro. . .

CONCLUDING PRAYER

60　The minister says a concluding prayer.

Father,
your Son accepted our sufferings
to teach us the virtue of patience in human illness.
Hear the prayers we offer for our sick brother/sister.
May all who suffer pain, illness, or disease
realize that they have been chosen to be saints
and know that they are joined to Christ
in his suffering for the salvation of the world.

We ask this through Christ our Lord.

R. Amen.

BLESSING

61　The minister may give a blessing.

All praise and glory is yours, Lord our God,
for you have called us to serve you in love.
Bless N.
so that he/she may bear this illness
in union with your Son's obedient suffering.
Restore him/her to health,
and lead him/her to glory.

We ask this through Christ our Lord.

R. Amen.

If the minister is a priest or deacon, he immediately concludes:

May the blessing of almighty God,
the Father, and the Son, + and the Holy Spirit,
come upon you and remain with you for ever.

R. Amen.

ORACION CONCLUSIVA

60. El ministro dice la oración conclusiva.

Padre nuestro,
tu Hijo aceptó nuestros sufrimientos
para enseñarnos la virtud de la paciencia en el dolor humano.
Escucha las oraciones que te ofrecemos
por nuestro (a) hermano(a) enfermo(a).
Que todos los que sufren dolores, enfermedades o males
se den cuenta de que han sido escogidos para ser santos
y para conocer que están unidos a Cristo,
que sufre por la salvación del mundo.
Te lo pedimos por Cristo, nuestro Señor.
R. Amén.

BENDICION

61. El ministro puede dar la bendición con la siguiénte fórmula:

Tú eres digno de toda gloria y alabanza, Señor, Dios nuestro,
porque tú nos has llamado a servirte amándote.
Bendice a N.,
para que él (ella) pueda sobrellevar su enfermedad,
en unión con los sufrimientos de tu Hijo, siempre obediente.
Devuélvele la salud,
y condúcelo(a) a la gloria.
Te lo pedimos por Cristo, nuestro Señor.
R. Amén.

Si el ministro es sacerdote o diácono, prosigue inmediatamente:

La bendición de Dios todopoderoso,
Padre, Hijo + y Espíritu Santo,
descienda sobre ti (ustedes)
y permanezca para siempre.
R. Amén,

The priest may lay hands upon the sick person's head.

A minister who is not a priest or deacon invokes God's blessing and makes the sign of the cross on himself or herself, while saying:

May the Lord bless us,
protect us from all evil,
and bring us to everlasting life.

R. Amen.

The minister may then trace the sign of the cross on the sick person's forehead.

El sacerdote puede imponerle las manos a la persona enferma.

Si el ministro no es ni sacerdote ni diácono, invoca la bendición de Dios haciendo sobre sí mismo(a) la señal de la cruz, y diciendo:

Que el Señor nos bendiga,
nos libre de todo mal
y nos lleve a la vida eterna.
R.   Amén.

Entonces el ministro puede trazar la señal de la cruz en la frente de la persona enferma.

Chapter Three

COMMUNION OF THE SICK

Chapter Three

COMMUNION OF THE SICK

INTRODUCTION

Whoever eats this bread will live for ever.

71   This chapter contains two rites: one for use when communion can be celebrated in the context of a liturgy of the word; the other, a brief communion rite for use in more restrictive circumstances, such as in hospitals.

72   Priests with pastoral responsibilities should see to it that the sick or aged, even though not seriously ill or in danger of death, are given every opportunity to receive the eucharist frequently, even daily, especially during the Easter season. They may receive communion at any hour. Those who care for the sick may receive communion with them, in accord with the usual norms. To provide frequent communion for the sick, it may be necessary to ensure that the community has a sufficient number of ministers of communion. The communion minister should wear attire appropriate to this ministry.

   The sick person and others may help to plan the celebration, for example, by choosing the prayers and readings. Those making these choices should keep in mind the condition of the sick person. The readings and the homily should help those present to reach a deeper understanding of the mystery of human suffering in relation to the paschal mystery of Christ.

73   The faithful who are ill are deprived of their rightful and accustomed place in the eucharistic community. In bringing communion to them the minister of communion represents Christ and manifests faith and charity on behalf of the whole community toward those who cannot be present at the eucharist. For the sick the reception of communion is not only a privilege but also a sign of support and concern shown by the Christian community for its members who are ill.

   The links between the community's eucharistic celebration, especially on the Lord's Day, and the communion of the sick are intimate and manifold. Besides remembering the sick in the general intercessions at Mass, those present should be reminded occasionally of the significance of communion in the lives of those who are ill: union with Christ in his struggle with evil, his prayer for the world, and his love for the Father, and union with the community from which they are separated.

The obligation to visit and comfort those who cannot take part in the eucharistic assembly may be clearly demonstrated by taking communion to them from the community's eucharistic celebration. This symbol of unity between the community and its sick members has the deepest significance on the Lord's Day, the special day of the eucharistic assembly.

74   When the eucharist is brought to the sick, it should be caried in a pyx or small closed container. Those who are with the sick should be asked to prepare a table covered with a linen cloth upon which the blessed sacrament will be placed. Lighted candles are prepared and, where it is customary, a vessel of holy water. Care should be taken to make the occasion special and joyful.

Sick people who are unable to receive under the form of bread may receive under the form of wine alone. If the wine is consecrated at a Mass not celebrated in the presence of the sick person, the blood of the Lord is kept in a properly covered vessel and is placed in the tabernacle after communion. The precious blood should be carried to the sick in a vessel which is closed in such a way as to eliminate all danger of spilling. If some of the precious blood remains, it should be consumed by the minister, who should also see to it that the vessel is properly purified.

75   If the sick wish to celebrate the sacrament of penance, it is preferable that the priest make himself available for this during a previous visit.

76   If it is necessary to celebrate the sacrament of penance during the rite of communion, it takes the place of the penitential rite.

COMMUNION IN ORDINARY CIRCUMSTANCES

77   If possible, provision should be made to celebrate Mass in the homes of the sick, with their families and friends gathered around them. The Ordinary determines the conditions and requirements for such celebrations.

COMMUNION IN A HOSPITAL OR INSTITUTION

78   There will be situations, particularly in large institutions with many communicants, when the minister should consider alternative means so that the rite of communion of the sick is not diminished to the absolute minimum. In such cases the following alternatives should be considered: (a) where possible, the residents or patients may be gathered in groups in one or more areas; (b) additional ministers of communion may assist.

When it is not possible to celebrate the full rite, the rite for communion in a hospital or institution may be used. If it is convenient, however, the minister may add elements from the rite for ordinary circumstances, for example, a Scripture reading.

79   The rite begins with the recitation of the eucharistic antiphon in the church, the hospital chapel, or the first room visited. Then the minister gives communion to the sick in their individual rooms.

80   The concluding prayer may be said in the church, the hospital chapel, or the last room visited. No blessing is given.

COMMUNION IN ORDINARY CIRCUMSTANCES

OUTLINE OF THE RITE

INTRODUCTORY RITES
Greeting
Sprinkling with Holy Water
Penitential Rite

LITURGY OF THE WORD
Reading
Response
General Intercessions

LITURGY OF HOLY COMMUNION
Lord's Prayer
Communion
Silent Prayer
Prayer after Communion

CONCLUDING RITE
Blessing

COMUNION EN CIRCUNSTANCIAS ORDINARIAS

ESQUEMA DEL RITO

RITOS INTRODUCTORIOS
Saludo
Aspersión con agua bendita
Rito penitencial

LITURGIA DE LA PALABRA
Lectura
Respuesta a la Palabra
Preces

LITURGIA DE LA COMUNION
Padrenuestro
Comunión
Oración en silencio
Oración después de la comunión

RITO CONCLUSIVO
Bendición

COMMUNION IN ORDINARY CIRCUMSTANCES

INTRODUCTORY RITES

GREETING

81   The minister greets the sick person and the others present.

The peace of the Lord be with you always.

R.   And also with you.

The minister then places the blessed sacrament on the table, and all join in adoration.

SPRINKLING WITH HOLY WATER

82   If it seems desirable, the priest or deacon may sprinkle the sick person and those present with holy water.

Let this water call to mind our baptism into Christ,
who by his death and resurrection has redeemed us.

If the sacrament of penance is now celebrated, the penitential rite is omitted.

COMUNION EN CIRCUNSTANCIAS
ORDINARIAS

RITOS INTRODUCTORIOS

SALUDO

81.   El ministro saluda a la persona enferma y a los presentes.

La paz del Señor esté siempre con ustedes.
R. Y también contigo.

Entonces el ministro coloca el Santísimo Sacramento en la mesa y todos juntos lo adoran.

ASPERSION CON AGUA BENDITA

82.   Si parece conveniente, el sacerdote o el diácono rocía con agua bendita a la persona enferma y a todos los presentes.

Que esta agua bendita nos recuerde
el bautismo que recibimos
y renueve nuestra fe en Cristo,
que con su muerte y resurrección nos redimió.

Si tiene lugar aquí el sacramento de la penitencia, se omite el rito penitencial.

PENITENTIAL RITE

83   The minister invites the sick person and all present to join in the penitential rite, using these or similar words:

My brothers and sisters, to prepare ourselves for this celebration, let us call to mind our sins.

After a brief period of silence, the penitential rite continues.

Lord Jesus, you healed the sick:
Lord, have mercy.

R. Lord, have mercy.

Lord Jesus, you forgave sinners:
Christ, have mercy.

R. Christ, have mercy.

Lord Jesus, you give us yourself to heal us
    and bring us strength:
Lord, have mercy.

R. Lord, have mercy.

The minister concludes the penitential rite with the following:

May almighty God have mercy on us,
forgive us our sins,
and bring us to everlasting life.

R. Amen.

RITO PENITENCIAL

83.   El ministro invita a la persona enferma y a todos los presentes a participar en el rito penitencial, con estas u otras palabras parecidas:

> Hermanos y hermanas,
> para prepararnos a esta celebración,
> reconozcamos nuestros pecados.

Después de un breve momento de silencio, prosigue el rito penitencial.

> Señor Jesús, que curaste a los enfermos:
> Señor, ten piedad de nosotros.
> R.   Señor, ten piedad de nosotros.
>
> Señor Jesús, que perdonaste a los pecadores:
> Cristo, ten piedad de nosotros.
> R.   Cristo, ten piedad de nosotros.
>
> Señor Jesús, que te entregaste a la muerte
> para sanarnos y darnos fortaleza:
> Señor, ten piedad de nosotros.
> R.   Señor ten piedad de nosotros.

El ministro concluye el rito penitencial, diciendo:

> El Señor todopoderoso tenga misericordia de nosotros,
> perdone nuestros pecados
> y nos lleve a la vida eterna.
> R.   Amén.

LITURGY OF THE WORD

READING

84   The word of God is proclaimed by one of those present or by the minister.

A reading from the holy gospel
according to John   6:51

Jesus says:
"I am the living bread which has come down from heaven.
Anyone who eats this bread will live for ever;
and the bread that I shall give
is my flesh, for the life of the world."

This is the Gospel of the Lord.

RESPONSE

85   A brief period of silence may be observed after the reading of the word of
God.

The minister may then give a brief explanation of the reading, applying it to the
needs of the sick person and those who are looking after him or her.

GENERAL INTERCESSIONS

86   The general intercessions may be said. With a brief introduction the
minister invites all those present to pray. After the intentions the minister says
the concluding prayer. It is desirable that the intentions be announced by
someone other than the minister.

LITURGIA DE LA PALABRA

LECTURA

84.   Uno de los presentes o el ministro proclama la palabra de Dios.

Lectura del santo Evangelio según San Juan   6.51

Jesús dice:
"Yo soy el pan vivo bajado del cielo,
el que coma de este pan vivirá para siempre.
El pan que yo daré es mi carne, y la daré
para la vida del mundo".

Esta es palabra de Dios.

RESPUESTA A LA PALABRA

85.   Se puede guardar un breve espacio de silencio, después de la lectura de
la palabra de Dios.

El ministro podrá explicar brevemente la lectura y aplicarla a las necesidades
de la persona enferma y de los que cuidan de ella.

PRECES

86.   Se pueden enunciar las peticiones generales. Mediante una breve introducción, el ministro invita a todos a orar. Después de las intenciones, el ministro recita la oración conclusiva. Es recomendable que una persona distinta
del ministro pronuncie las intenciones.

LITURGY OF HOLY COMMUNION

LORD'S PRAYER

87   The minister introduces the Lord's Prayer in these or similar words:

Now let us pray as Christ the Lord has taught us:

All say:

Our Father . . .

COMMUNION

88   The minister shows the eucharistic bread to those present, saying:

This is the bread of life.
Taste and see that the Lord is good.

The sick person and all who are to receive communion say:

Lord, I am not worthy to receive you,
but only say the word and I shall be healed.

The minister goes to the sick person and, showing the blessed sacrament, says:

The body of Christ.

The sick person answers: "Amen," and receives communion.

Then the minister says:

The blood of Christ.

The sick person answers: "Amen," and receives communion.

Others present who wish to receive communion then do so in the usual way.

After the conclusion of the rite, the minister cleanses the vessel as usual.

LITURGIA DE LA COMUNION

PADRENUESTRO

87. El ministro introduce la oración del Señor con estas u otras palabras similares:

Oremos confiadamente al Padre con las palabras
que nos enseñó nuestro Salvador:

Todos dicen:

Padre nuestro. . .

COMUNION

88. El ministro presenta el pan eucarístico a los presentes, con estas palabras:

Este es el pan de la vida.
Prueben y vean qué bueno es el Señor.

La persona enferma y todos los que vayan a recibir la comunión dicen:

Señor, yo no soy digno de que vengas a mí,
pero una palabra tuya bastará para sanarme.

El ministro se acerca a la persona enferma y presentándole la sagrada forma, dice:

El Cuerpo de Cristo.

La persona enferma responde "Amén" y recibe la comunión. Enseguida el ministro dice:

La Sangre de Cristo.

La persona enferma responde: "Amén" y recibe la comunión.

Si algunas otras personas presentes quieren comulgar, lo hacen en la forma acostumbrada.

Terminado el rito, el ministro purifica los vasos sagrados, como de costumbre.

SILENT PRAYER

89   Then a period of silence may be observed.

PRAYER AFTER COMMUNION

90   The minister says a concluding prayer.

Let us pray.

Pause for silent prayer, if this has not preceded.

God our Father,
you have called us to share the one bread and one cup
and so become one in Christ.

Help us to live in him
that we may bear fruit,
rejoicing that he has redeemed the world.

We ask this through Christ our Lord.

R. Amen.

CONCLUDING RITE

BLESSING

91   The priest or deacon blesses the sick person and the others present. If, however, any of the blessed sacrament remains, he may bless the sick person by making a sign of the cross with the blessed sacrament, in silence.

May God the Father bless you.
R. Amen.
May God the Son heal you.
R. Amen.
May God the Holy Spirit enlighten you.
R. Amen.
May almighty God bless you,
the Father, and the Son, + and the Holy Spirit.
R. Amen.

ORACION EN SILENCIO

89.   Se puede orar aquí en silencio.

ORACION DESPUES DE LA COMUNION

90.   El ministro reza la oración conclusiva.

Oremos.

Pausa para orar en silencio, si no se ha hecho anteriormente.

Señor y Padre nuestro,
que nos has llamado a participar
del mismo pan y del mismo vino,
para vivir así unidos a Cristo,
Ayúdanos a vivir unidos a él,
para que produzcamos fruto,
experimentando el gozo de su redención.
Por Cristo, nuestro Señor.
R.   Amén.

RITO CONCLUSIVO

BENDICION

91.   El sacerdote o el diácono bendice a la persona enferma y a los presentes. Pero, en el caso de que hayan quedado algunas formas consagradas, puede bendecir al enfermo, haciendo, en silencio, la señal de la cruz con el Santísimo Sacramento.

Que Dios Padre te bendiga.
R.   Amén.
Que Dios Hijo te cure.
R.   Amén.
Que Dios Espíritu Santo te ilumine.
R.   Amén.

Que te bendiga Dios todopoderoso,
Padre, Hijo +y Espíritu Santo.
R.   Amén.

A minister who is not a priest or deacon invokes God's blessing and makes the sign of the cross on himself or herself, while saying:

May the Lord bless us,
protect us from all evil,
and bring us to everlasting life.

R. Amen.

Si el ministro no es sacerdote ni diácono, invoca la bendición de Dios y hace sobre sí mismo(a) la señal de la cruz, diciendo:

Que el Señor nos bendiga,
nos libre de todo mal
y nos lleve a la vida eterna.
R.   Amén.

COMMUNION IN A HOSPITAL OR INSTITUTION

OUTLINE OF THE RITE

INTRODUCTORY RITE
Antiphon

LITURGY OF HOLY COMMUNION
Greeting
Lord's Prayer
Communion

CONCLUDING RITE
Concluding Prayer

COMUNION EN UN HOSPITAL U OTRA INSTITUCION

ESQUEMA DEL RITO

RITO INTRODUCTORIO
Antífona

LITURGIA DE LA COMUNION
Saludo
Padrenuestro
Comunión

RITO CONCLUSIVO

Oración final

COMMUNION IN A HOSPITAL
OR INSTITUTION

INTRODUCTORY RITE

ANTIPHON

92   The rite may begin in the church, the hospital chapel, or the first room, where the minister says the following antiphon:

How holy this feast
in which Christ is our food:
his passion is recalled;
grace fills our hearts;
and we receive a pledge of the glory to come.

If it is customary, the minister may be accompanied by a person carrying a candle.

LITURGY OF HOLY COMMUNION

GREETING

93   On entering each room, the minister may use the following greeting:

The peace of the Lord be with you always.

R.   And also with you.

The minister then places the blessed sacrament on the table, and all join in adoration.

If there is time and it seems desirable, the minister may proclaim a Scripture reading.

COMUNION EN UN HOSPITAL

U OTRA INSTITUCION

RITO INTRODUCTORIO

ANTIFONA

92. El rito puede iniciarse en el templo, en la capilla del hospital o en el primer cuarto, en donde el sacerdote recita la siguiente antífona:

¡Oh sagrado banquete
donde Cristo es alimento!
Se recuerda su pasión,
el alma se llena de gracia
y se nos da en prenda
la gloria futura.

Si se acostumbra, el ministro puede ir acompañado por una persona que lleve una vela.

LITURGIA DE LA COMUNION

SALUDO

93. Al entrar en cada habitación, el ministro puede recitar el siguiente saludo:

Que la paz del Señor esté siempre con ustedes.
R.   Y también contigo.

El ministro coloca el Santísimo Sacramento en la mesa y todos juntos lo adoran.

Si hay tiempo y parece conveniente, el ministro puede proclamar la palabra.

LORD'S PRAYER

94   When circumstances permit (for example, when there are not many rooms to visit), the minister is encouraged to lead the sick in the Lord's Prayer. The minister introduces the Lord's Prayer in these or similar words:

Jesus taught us to call God our Father, and so we have the courage to say:

All say:

Our Father . . .

COMMUNION

95   The minister shows the eucharistic bread to those present, saying:

This is the Lamb of God
who takes away the sins of the world.
Happy are those who hunger and thirst,
for they shall be satisfied.

The sick person and all who are to receive communion say:

Lord, I am not worthy to receive you,
but only say the word and I shall be healed.

The minister goes to the sick person and, showing the blessed sacrament, says:

The body of Christ.

The sick person answers: "Amen," and receives communion.

Then the minister says:

The blood of Christ.

The sick person answers: "Amen," and receives communion.

Others present who wish to receive communion then do so in the usual way.

PADRENUESTRO

94.   Si las circunstancias lo permiten (por ejemplo,si no son muchas las salas que hay que visitar), es muy conveniente que el ministro guíe a los enfermos en la recitación del padrenuestro. Puede hacerlo con éstas o semejantes palabras:

> Jesús nos enseñó a llamar Padre a Dios;
> por eso nos atrevemos a decir:

Todos dicen:

Padre nuestro. . .

COMUNION

95.   El ministro muestra el pan eucarístico a los presentes, diciendo:

> Este es el Cordero de.Dios
> que quita el pecado del mundo.
> ¡Dichosos los que tienen hambre y sed,
> porque ellos están saciados!

La persona enferma y todos aquellos que vayan a comulgar dicen:

Señor, yo no soy digno de que vengas a mí,
pero una palabra tuya bastará para sanarme.

El ministro se acerca a la persona enferma, le muestra la hostia, diciéndole:

El Cuerpo de Cristo.

La persona enferma responde: "Amén", y recibe la comunión.
Entonces el ministro dice:

La Sangre de Cristo.

La persona enferma responde: "Amén", y recibe la comunión.

Las demás personas que quieran comulgar reciben la comunión en la forma acostumbrada.

CONCLUDING RITE

CONCLUDING PRAYER

96   The concluding prayer may be said either in the last room visited, in the church, or chapel.

Let us pray.

Pause for silent prayer.

God our Father,
you have called us to share the one bread and one cup
and so become one in Christ.

Help us to live in him
that we may bear fruit,
rejoicing that he has redeemed the world.

We ask this through Christ our Lord.

R. Amen.

The blessing is omitted and the minister cleanses the vessel as usual.

RITO CONCLUSIVO

ORACION CONCLUSIVA

96.   La oración conclusiva puede recitarse en el último salón o habitación o en la iglesia o en la capilla.

Oremos.

Pausa para orar en silencio.

> Señor y Padre nuestro,
> que nos has llamado a participar
> del mismo pan y del mismo vino,
> para vivir así unidos a Cristo,
> ayúdanos a vivir unidos a él,
> para que produzcamos fruto,
> experimentando el gozo de su redención.
> Por Cristo, nuestro Señor.
> R.   Amén.

Se omite la bendición y el ministro purifica los vasos sagrados como de costumbre.

Chapter Four

ANOINTING OF THE SICK

Chapter Four

ANOINTING OF THE SICK

INTRODUCTION

Do not be worried or distressed. Have faith in God, and faith in me.

97   The sacrament of anointing is the proper sacrament for those Christians whose health is seriously impaired by sickness or old age. It may be celebrated in the home, in a hospital or institution, or in church. This chapter contains three rites for use in these varying circumstances: anointing outside Mass, anointing within Mass, and anointing in a hospital or institution. Several sick persons may be anointed within the rite especially if the celebration takes place in a church or hospital. While the sacrament will be celebrated more frequently outside Mass, the celebration may also take place within Mass.

98   In the course of his visits to the sick, the priest should try to explain two complementary aspects of this sacrament: through the sacrament of anointing the Church supports the sick in their struggle against illness and continues Christ's messianic work of healing. All who are united in the bond of a common baptism and a common faith are joined together in the body of Christ since what happens to one member affects all. The sacrament of anointing effectively expresses the share that each one has in the sufferings of others. When the priest anoints the sick, he is anointing in the name and with the power of Christ himself (see Mark 6:13). On behalf of the whole community, he is ministering to those members who are suffering. This message of hope and comfort is also needed by those who care for the sick, especially those who are closely bound in love to them. There should be opportunity for suitable preparation over a period of time for the benefit of the sick themselves and of those who are with them.

99   The priest should ensure that the abuse of delaying the reception of the sacrament does not occur, and that the celebration takes place while the sick person is capable of active participation. However, the intent of the conciliar reform (Constitution on the Liturgy, art. 73) that those needing the sacrament should seek it at the beginning of a serious illness should not be used to anoint those who are not proper subjects for the sacrament. The sacrament of the

anointing of the sick should be celebrated only when a Christian's health is seriously impaired by sickness or old age.

Because of its very nature as a sign, the sacrament of the anointing of the sick should be celebrated with members of the family and other representatives of the Christian community whenever this is possible. Then the sacrament is seen for what it is — a part of the prayer of the Church and an encounter with the Lord. The sign of the sacrament will be further enhanced by avoiding undue haste in prayer and action.

100 The priest should inquire about the physical and spiritual condition of the sick person and he should become acquainted with the family, friends, and others who may be present. The sick person and others may help to plan the celebration, for example, by choosing the readings and prayers. It will be especially helpful if the sick person, the priest, and the family become accustomed to praying together.

In the choice of readings the condition of the sick person should be kept in mind. The readings and the homily should help those present to reach a deeper understanding of the mystery of human suffering in relation to the paschal mystery of Christ.

The sick person who is not confined to bed may take part in the sacrament of anointing in a church, chapel, or other appropriate place. He or she should be made comfortable and there should be room for relatives and friends. In hospitals and other institutions the priest should consider all who will be present for the celebration: whether they are able to take part; whether they are very weak; and, if they are not Catholic, whether they might be offended.

101 If the sick person wishes to celebrate the sacrament of penance, it is preferable that the priest make himself available for this during a previous visit. If it is necessary to celebrate the sacrament of penance during the rite of anointing, it takes the place of the penitential rite. The priest should also arrange for the continued pastoral care of the sick, especially for frequent opportunities to receive communion.

102 The sacrament of anointing may be repeated:

a)   when the sick person recovers after being anointed and, at a later time, becomes sick again;

b)   when during the same illness the condition of the sick person becomes more serious.

In the case of a person who is chronically ill, or elderly and in a weakened condition, the sacrament of anointing may be repeated when in the pastoral judgment of the priest the condition of the sick person warrants the repetition of the sacrament.

103 A sick person who recovers after being anointed should be encouraged to give thanks for the favors received, especially by participating in a Mass of thanksgiving.

CELEBRATING THE SACRAMENT OF ANOINTING

104 There are three distinct and integral aspects to the celebration of this sacrament: the prayer of faith, the laying on of hands, and the anointing with oil.

105 *Prayer of faith:* The community, asking God's help for the sick, makes its prayer of faith in response to God's word and in a spirit of trust (see James 5:14-15). In the rites for the sick, it is the people of God who pray in faith. The entire Church is made present in this community — represented by at least the priest, family, friends, and others — assembled to pray for those to be anointed. If they are able, the sick persons should also join in this prayer.

106 *Laying on of hands:* The gospels contain a number of instances in which Jesus healed the sick by the laying on of hands or even by the simple gesture of touch. The ritual has restored to major significance the gesture of the laying on of hands with its several meanings. With this gesture the priest indicates that this particular person is the object of the Church's prayer of faith. The laying on of hands is clearly a sign of blessing, as we pray that by the power of God's healing grace the sick person may be restored to health or at least strengthened in time of illness. The laying on of hands is also an invocation: the Church prays for the coming of the Holy Spirit upon the sick person. Above all, it is the biblical gesture of healing and indeed Jesus' own usual manner of healing: "They brought the sick with various diseases to him; and he laid hands on every one of them and healed them" (Luke 4:40).

107 *Anointing with oil:* The practice of anointing the sick with oil signifies healing, strengthening, and the presence of the Spirit.
   In the gospel of Mark the disciples were sent out by the Lord to continue his healing ministry: "They anointed many sick people with oil and cured them" (Mark 6:13). And Saint James witnesses to the fact that the Church continued to anoint the sick with oil as both a means and sign of healing (James 5:14). The Church's use of oil for healing is closely related to its remedial use in soothing and comforting the sick and in restoring the tired and the weak. Thus the sick person is strengthened to fight against the physically and spiritually debilitating effects of illness. The prayer for blessing the oil of the sick reminds us, furthermore, that the oil of anointing is the sacramental sign of the presence, power, and grace of the Holy Spirit.

If the anointing is to be an effective sacramental symbol, there should be a generous use of oil so that it will be seen and felt by the sick person as a sign of the Spirit's healing and strengthening presence. For the same reason, it is not desirable to wipe off the oil after the anointing.

ANOINTING OF THE SICK
WITH A LARGE CONGREGATION

108 The rites for anointing outside Mass and anointing within Mass may be used to anoint a number of people within the same celebration. These rites are appropriate for large gatherings of a diocese, parish, or society for the sick, or for pilgrimages. These celebrations should take place in a church, chapel, or other appropriate place where the sick and others can easily gather. On occasion, they may also take place in hospitals and other institutions.

If the diocesan bishop decides that many people are to be anointed in the same celebration, either he or his delegate should ensure that all disciplinary norms concerning anointing are observed, as well as the norms for pastoral preparation and liturgical celebration. In particular, the practice of indiscriminately anointing numbers of people on these occasions simply because they are ill or have reached an advanced age is to be avoided. Only those whose health is seriously impaired by sickness or old age are proper subjects for the sacrament. The diocesan bishop also designates the priests who will take part in the celebration of the sacrament.

The full participation of those present must be fostered by every means, especially through the use of appropriate songs, so that the celebration manifests the Easter joy which is proper to this sacrament.

109 The communal rite begins with a greeting followed by a reception of the sick, which is a sympathetic expression of Christ's concern for those who are ill and of the role of the sick in the people of God.

Before the rite of dismissal the blessing is given. The celebration may conclude with an appropriate song.

110 If there are large numbers of sick people to be anointed, other priests may assist the celebrant. Each priest lays hands on some of the sick and anoints them, using the sacramental form. Everything else is done once for all, and the prayers are said in the plural by the celebrant. After the sacramental form has been heard at least once by those present, suitable songs may be sung while the rest of the sick are being anointed.

ANOINTING OUTSIDE MASS

INTRODUCTION

He has borne our sickness and endured our suffering.

111 The rite which follows provides for the celebration of the sacrament of anointing outside Mass. This celebration takes place in the home, in a hospital or institution, or in church. Appropriate vestments should be worn by the priest.

112 The priest should inquire beforehand about the physical and spiritual condition of the sick person and he should become acquainted with the family, friends, and others who may be present. If possible, he should involve them in the preparation for the celebration, for example, in the choice of the readings and prayers, and he should explain to them the significance of the sacrament. Since the liturgical texts appear in the singular, they must be adapted in gender and number for a celebration in which two or more people are anointed.

113 If the sick person wishes to celebrate the sacrament of penance, it is preferable that the priest make himself available for this during a previous visit. If it is necessary for the sick person to confess during the celebration of the sacrament of anointing, this takes the place of the penitential rite.

114 If communion is to be given during the celebration, this occurs after the liturgy of anointing.

ANOINTING OUTSIDE MASS

OUTLINE OF THE RITE

INTRODUCTORY RITES
Greeting
Sprinkling with Holy Water
Instruction
Penitential Rite

LITURGY OF THE WORD
Reading
Response

LITURGY OF ANOINTING
Litany
Laying on of Hands
Prayer over the Oil
Anointing
Prayer after Anointing
Lord's Prayer

[LITURGY OF HOLY COMMUNION]
Communion
Silent Prayer
Prayer after Communion

CONCLUDING RITE
Blessing

UNCION FUERA DE LA MISA

ESQUEMA DEL RITO

RITOS INTRODUCTORIOS
Saludo
Aspersión con agua bendita
Instrucción
Rito penitencial

LITURGIA DE LA PALABRA
Lectura
Respuesta a la Palabra

LITURGIA DE LA UNCION
Letanías
Imposición de las manos
Bendición del óleo
Unción
Oración después de la unción
Padrenuestro

LITURGIA DE LA COMUNION
Comunión
Oración en silencio
Oración después de la comunión

RITO CONCLUSIVO
Bendición

ANOINTING OUTSIDE MASS

INTRODUCTORY RITES

GREETING

115 The priest greets the sick person and the others present.

The peace of the Lord be with you always.

R. And also with you.

If communion is to take place during the rite, the priest then places the blessed sacrament on the table, and all join in adoration.

SPRINKLING WITH HOLY WATER

116 If it seems desirable, the priest may sprinkle the sick person and those present with holy water.

The Lord is our shepherd
and leads us to streams of living water.

INSTRUCTION

117 Then he addresses those present in these or similar words:

My dear friends, we are gathered here in the name of our Lord Jesus Christ who is present among us. As the gospels relate, the sick came to him for healing; moreover he loves us so much that he died for our sake. Through the apostle James, he has commanded us: "Are there any who are sick among you? Let them send for the priests of the Church, and let the priests pray over them, anointing them with oil in the name of the Lord; and the prayer of faith will save the sick persons, and the Lord will raise them up; and if they have committed any sins, their sins will be forgiven them." (James 5:14–15)

UNCION FUERA DE LA MISA

RITOS INTRODUCTORIOS

SALUDO

115. El sacerdote saluda a la persona enferma y a todos los presentes.

La paz del Señor esté siempre con ustedes.
R. Y también contigo.

Si la persona enferma va a recibir la comunión durante el rito de la unción, entonces el sacerdote coloca el Santísimo Sacramento en la mesa y todos lo adoran.

ASPERSION CON AGUA BENDITA

116. Si parece conveniente, el sacerdote rocía con agua bendita a la persona enferma y a los presentes.

El Señor es nuestro pastor,
él nos conduce a los manantiales de la vida.

INSTRUCCION

117. Enseguida dirige a los presentes las siguientes palabras u otras semejantes.

Hermanos: Estamos reunidos aquí en nombre de nuestro Señor Jesucristo, que está presente con nosotros. Los Evangelios relatan que los enfermos se acercaban a Jesús para que los curara. Y no solamente los curó a ellos, sino que quiere curarnos a todos, porque a todos nos ama, y por eso precisamente murió en la cruz. Nuestro Señor nos enseña, por medio de Santiago Apóstol, la verdad y eficacia de la unción de los enfermos, con estas palabras: "Hermanos: El que esté enfermo, que llame a los presbíteros de la Iglesia para que rueguen por él, ungiéndolo con aceite en nombre del Señor. La oración hecha con fe salvará al enfermo; el Señor los levantará y, si ha cometido pecados, le serán perdonados". (Sant. 5, 14-15)

Let us therefore commend our sick brother/sister N. to the grace and power of Christ, that he may save him/her and raise him/her up.

If the sacrament of penance is now celebrated, the penitential rite is omitted.

PENITENTIAL RITE

118   The priest invites the sick person and all present to join in the penitential rite, using these or similar words:

My brothers and sisters, to prepare ourselves for this holy anointing, let us call to mind our sins.

After a brief period of silence, the penitential rite continues.

All say:

> I confess to almighty God,
> and to you, my brothers and sisters,
> that I have sinned through my own fault

They strike their breast.

> in my thoughts and in my words,
> in what I have done,
> and in what I have failed to do;
> and I ask blessed Mary, ever virgin,
> all the angels and saints,
> and you, my brothers and sisters,
> to pray for me to the Lord our God.

The priest concludes the penitential rite with the following:

May almighty God have mercy on us,
forgive us our sins,
and bring us to everlasting life.

R. Amen.

Encomendemos, pues, a nuestro(a) hermano(a) enfermo(a) a Cristo, nuestro Señor, lleno de poder y de gracia, para que lo(a) salve y lo(a) cure.

Si se celebra el sacramento de la penitencia, se omite el rito penitencial.

RITO PENITENCIAL

118. El sacerdote invita a la persona enferma y a todos los presentes a participar en el rito penitencial. Puede hacerlo con la exhortación que va a continuación o con otras parecidas:

Hermanos y hermanas, preparémonos para la sagrada unción, reconociendo nuestros pecados.

Después de un corto tiempo de silencio, se prosigue el rito penitencial.

Todos dicen:

Yo confieso ante Dios todopoderoso
y ante ustedes, hermanos,
que he pecado mucho,
de pensamiento, palabra, obra y omisión;
por mi culpa, por mi culpa, por mi gran culpa.

Se golpean el pecho.

Por eso ruego a santa María, siempre virgen,
a los ángeles, a los santos
y a ustedes, hermanos,
que intercedan por mí ante Dios, nuestro Señor.

El sacerdote concluye el rito penitencial con las siguientes palabras:

Dios todopoderoso tenga misericordia de nosotros,
perdone nuestros pecados
y nos lleve a la vida eterna.
R.   Amén.

LITURGY OF THE WORD

READING

119 The word of God is proclaimed by one of those present or by the priest.

A reading from the holy gospel
according to Matthew   11:25-30

Childlike confidence in the goodness of God will bring us the "rest" that only Jesus can give.

At that time Jesus exclaimed, "I bless you, Father, Lord of heaven and of earth, for hiding these things from the learned and the clever and revealing them to mere children. Yes, Father, for that is what it pleased you to do. Everything has been entrusted to me by my Father and no one knows the Son except the Father, just as no one knows the Father except the Son and those to whom the Son chooses to reveal him.

"Come to me, all you who labor and are overburdened, and I will give you rest. Shoulder my yoke and learn from me, for I am gentle and humble in heart, and you will find rest for your souls. Yes, my yoke is easy and my burden light."

This is the Gospel of the Lord.

RESPONSE

120 A brief period of silence may be observed after the reading of the word of God.

The priest may then give a brief explanation of the reading, applying it to the needs of the sick person and those who are looking after him or her.

LITURGIA DE LA PALABRA

LECTURA

119. El sacerdote o uno de los presentes proclama la palabra de Dios.

Lectura del santo Evangelio según san Mateo   11, 25-30

La confianza de niños en la bondad de Dios nos permitirá,
encontrar el descanso que sólo Jesús puede dar.

Por aquel tiempo exclamó Jesús: "Padre, Señor del cielo y de la tierra,
yo te alabo porque has mantenido ocultas estas cosas a los sabios y
prudentes y las revelaste a la gente sencilla. Sí, Padre, así te pareció
bien.

El Padre puso todas las cosas en mis manos. Nadie conoce al Hijo sino
el Padre, ni nadie conoce al Padre sino el Hijo y aquellos a los que el
Hijo quiere dárselo a conocer.

Vengan a mí los que se sienten cargados y agobiados, porque yo los
aliviaré. Carguen con mi yugo y aprendan de mí que soy paciente de
corazón y humilde, y sus almas encontrarán alivio. Pues mi yugo es
bueno y mi carga liviana".

Esta es palabra de Dios.

RESPUESTA A LA PALABRA

120. Después de la lectura de la palabra de Dios, se pueden guardar unos momentos de silencio.

A continuación el sacerdote puede explicar brevemente el Evangelio, aplicán-
dolo a las necesidades de la persona enferma y de los presentes.

LITURGY OF ANOINTING

LITANY

121 The priest may adapt or shorten the litany according to the condition of the sick person.

My brothers and sisters, in our prayer of faith let us appeal to God for our brother/sister N.

Come and strengthen him/her through this holy anointing: Lord have mercy.

R. Lord, have mercy.

Free him/her from all harm: Lord, have mercy.   R.

Free him/her from sin and all temptation: Lord have mercy.   R.

Relieve the sufferings of all the sick [here present]: Lord, have mercy.   R.

Assist all those dedicated to the care of the sick: Lord, have mercy.   R.

Give life and health to our brother/sister N., on whom we lay our hands in your name: Lord, have mercy.   R.

LAYING ON OF HANDS

122 In silence, the priest lays his hands on the head of the sick person.

LITURGIA DE LA UNCION

LETANIAS

121. El sacerdote puede adaptar, alargar o abreviar las letanías, de acuerdo con la condición de la persona enferma.

Hermanos y hermanas, con la oración de nuestra fe, invoquemos humildemente al Señor, y roguémosle por nuestro(a) hermano(a) N.

Muéstrale, Señor, tu misericordia y confórtalo por medio de esta santa unción.
R.   Te lo pedimos, Señor.

Líbralo(a) de todo mal.
R.   Te lo pedimos, Señor.

Libra a este(a) enfermo(a) de todo pecado y de toda tentación.
R.   Te lo pedimos, Señor.

Alivia los sufrimientos de todos los enfermos (de esta casa).
R.   Te lo pedimos, Señor.

Concede también tu gracia a todos los que se consagran al servicio de los enfermos.
R.   Te lo pedimos, Señor.

Concede vida y salud a este(a) enfermo(a), a quien vamos a imponer las manos en tu nombre.
R.   Te lo pedimos, Señor.

IMPOSICION DE LAS MANOS

122. El sacerdote, en silencio, le impone las manos en la cabeza a la persona enferma.

PRAYER OVER THE OIL

123   The priest says a prayer of thanksgiving over blessed oil or he may bless the oil himself (see no. 21), using one of the following:

THANKSGIVING OVER BLESSED OIL—If the oil is already blessed, the priest says the following prayer of thanksgiving over it:

Praise to you, God, the almighty Father.
You sent your Son to live among us
and bring us salvation.

R.   Blessed be God who heals us in Christ.

Praise to you, God, the only-begotten Son.
You humbled yourself to share in our humanity
and you heal our infirmities. R.

Praise to you, God, the Holy Spirit, the Consoler.
Your unfailing power gives us strength
in our bodily weakness.   R.

God of mercy,
ease the sufferings and comfort the weakness
   of your servant N.,
whom the Church anoints with this holy oil.

We ask this through Christ our Lord.

R.   Amen.

ORACION POR EL OLEO

123.   El sacerdote dice una oración de acción de gracias por el óleo bendecido con anterioridad (ver n. 21), con las siguientes palabras:

Acción de gracias por el óleo bendecido. Si el óleo ha sido bendecido anteriormente, el sacerdote dice la siguiente oración de acción de gracias.

Bendito seas, Dios Padre omnipotente,
que enviaste a tu Hijo al mundo,
por nosotros y por nuestra salvación.
R.   Bendito seas por siempre, Señor.

Bendito seas, Dios Hijo unigénito,
que, haciéndote hombre como nosotros,
quisiste aliviar nuestras enfermedades.
R.   Bendito seas por siempre, Señor.

Bendito seas, Dios Espíritu Santo consolador,
que con tu ilimitado poder
sanas la debilidad de nuestro cuerpo.
R.   Bendito seas por siempre, Señor.

Señor, concede alivio a los sufrimientos de este(a) hijo(a) tuyo(a),
que en ti cree, y que va ser ungido con el óleo santo; confórtalo(a)
en su enfermedad. Por Cristo, nuestro Señor.
R.   Amén.

BLESSING OF OIL—When the priest blesses the oil during the rite, he uses the following blessing:

Let us pray.

God of all consolation,
you chose and sent your Son to heal the world.
Graciously listen to our prayer of faith:
send the power of your Holy Spirit, the Consoler,
into this precious oil, this soothing ointment,
this rich gift, this fruit of the earth.

Bless this oil + and sanctify it for our use.

Make this oil a remedy for all who are anointed with it;
heal them in body, in soul, and in spirit,
and deliver them from every affliction.

We ask this through our Lord Jesus Christ, your Son,
who lives and reigns with you and the Holy Spirit,
one God, for ever and ever.

R. Amen.

Bendición del óleo. Cuando el sacerdote bendice el óleo durante la ceremonia, utiliza la siguiente fórmula:

Oremos.
Dios nuestro, Padre de todo consuelo,
que por medio de tu Hijo
quisiste curar las dolencias de los enfermos,
atiende benignamente la oración de nuestra fe.
Envía desde el cielo a tu Santo Espíritu Consolador
y bendice + con tu poder este óleo
que tú nos has dado para utilidad nuestra.
Te rogamos que los enfermos ungidos con él,
experimenten tu protección en el cuerpo y en el alma
y se sientan aliviados en su debilidad,
en sus dolores y enfermedades.
Que se convierta, pues, para nosotros, en óleo santo,
bendecido por ti en el nombre de nuestro Señor Jesucristo,
que vive y reina contigo por los siglos de los siglos.
R.   Amén.

ANOINTING

124 The priest anoints the sick person with the blessed oil.

First he anoints the forehead, saying:

Through this holy anointing
may the Lord in his love and mercy help you
with the grace of the Holy Spirit.

R. Amen.

Then he anoints the hands, saying:

May the Lord who frees you from sin
save you and raise you up.

R. Amen.

The sacramental form is said only once, for the anointing of the forehead and hands, and is not repeated.

Depending upon the culture and traditions of the place, as well as the condition of the sick person, the priest may also anoint additional parts of the body, for example, the area of pain or injury. He does not repeat the sacramental form.

PRAYER AFTER ANOINTING

125 The priest says the following prayer:

Let us pray.

Father in heaven,
through this holy anointing
grant N. comfort in his/her suffering.

When he/she is afraid, give him/her courage,
when afflicted, give him/her patience,
when dejected, afford him/her hope,
and when alone, assure him/her of the support
   of your holy people.

We ask this through Christ our Lord.

R. Amen.

UNCION

124. El sacerdote unge a la persona enferma con el aceite sagrado.

Le unge primero la frente, diciendo:

**POR ESTA SANTA UNCION
Y POR SU BONDADOSA MISERICORDIA
TE AYUDE EL SEÑOR CON LA GRACIA
DEL ESPIRITU SANTO.
R. Amén.**

Después unge las manos, diciendo:

**PARA QUE, LIBRE DE TUS PECADOS,
TE CONCEDA LA SALVACION
Y TE CONFORTE EN TU ENFERMEDAD.
R. Amén.**

La forma sacramental se dice una sola vez para la unción de la frente y las manos, y no se repite.

De acuerdo con la cultura y tradiciones del lugar, y teniendo también en cuenta la condición de la persona enferma, el sacerdote puede ungir también algunas otras partes del cuerpo, por ejemplo, la región del dolor o de la herida. Pero lo hace sin repetir la fórmula de la unción.

ORACION DESPUES DE LA UNCION

125. El sacerdote dice la siguiente oración:

Oremos

Padre celestial,
por medio de esta sagrada unción
dale a N. alivio en sus sufrimientos.

Cuando tenga miedo, concédele valor;
cuando se sienta afligido(a), dale paciencia;
cuando se sienta deprimido(a), concédele esperanza;
cuando se sienta solo(a), dale la compañía de tu pueblo santo

Te lo pedimos por Cristo, nuestro Señor.

R.   Amén.

LORDS PRAYER

126   The priest introduces the Lord's Prayer in these or similar words:

Now let us offer together the prayer our Lord Jesus Christ taught us:

All say:

Our Father . . .

If the sick person does not receive communion, the rite concludes with a blessing.

LITURGY OF HOLY COMMUNION

COMMUNION

127   The priest shows the eucharistic bread to those present, saying:

This is the Lamb of God
who takes away the sins of the world.
Come to me all you that labor and are burdened
and I will refresh you.

The sick person and all who are to receive communion say:

Lord, I am not worthy to receive you,
but only say the word and I shall be healed.

The priest goes to the sick person and, showing the blessed Sacrament, says:

The body of Christ.

The sick person answers: "Amen," and receives communion.

Then the priest says:

The blood of Christ.

The sick person answers: "Amen," and receives communion.

Others present who wish to receive communion then do so in the usual way.

After the conclusion of the rite, the priest cleanses the vessel as usual.

PADRENUESTRO

126. El sacerdote introduce el padrenuestro con estas palabras u otras parecidas:

Oremos como Cristo nuestro Señor nos enseñó:

Todos dicen:

Padre nuestro. . .

Si la persona enferma no va a comulgar, el rito concluye con la bendición.

LITURGIA DE LA SAGRADA COMUNION

COMUNION

127. El sacerdote muestra el pan eucarístico a los presentes, diciendo:

Este es el Cordero de Dios
que quita el pecado del mundo.
Vengan a mí, todos los que están fatigados
y agobiados por la carga,
y yo los aliviaré.

La persona enferma y todos los que vayan a comulgar dicen:

Señor, yo no soy digno de que vengas a mí,
pero una palabra tuya bastará para sanarme.

El sacerdote se acerca a la persona enferma, le muestra el Santísimo Sacramento, y le dice:

El Cuerpo de Cristo.

La persona enferma responde "Amén", y recibe la comunión.

Luego el sacerdote dice:

La Sangre de Cristo.

La persona enferma responde "Amén" y recibe la comunión.

Si otras personas quieren recibir la comunión, pueden hacerlo en la forma ordinaria.

Terminado el rito, el sacerdote purifica los vasos sagrados, como de costumbre.

SILENT PRAYER

128 Then a period of silence may be observed.

PRAYER AFTER COMMUNION

129 The priest says a concluding prayer.

Let us pray.

Pause for silent prayer, if this has not preceded.

All-powerful God,
through the paschal mystery of Christ your Son
you have completed the work of our redemption.

May we, who in these sacramental signs
proclaim his death and resurrection,
grow in the experience of your saving power.

We ask this through Christ our Lord.

R. Amen.

CONCLUDING RITE

BLESSING

130 The priest blesses the sick person and the others present.If, however, any of
the blessed sacrament remains, he may bless the sick person by making a sign of the
cross with the blessed sacrament, in silence.

May the Lord be with you to protect you.
R. Amen.

May he guide you and give you strength.
R. Amen.

May he watch over you, keep you in his care,
and bless you with his peace.
R. Amen.

May almighty God bless you,
the Father, and the Son, + and the Holy Spirit.
R. Amen.

ORACION EN SILENCIO

128. A continuación se puede guardar un momento de silencio.

ORACION DESPUES DE LA COMUNION

129. El sacerdote dice la oración conclusiva.

Oremos.
Pausa para orar en silencio, si no se ha hecho ya.

> Dios nuestro,
> que por el misterio pascual de tu Hijo unigénito,
> llevaste a plenitud la redención humana,
> concede a quienes anunciamos con fe
> la muerte y la resurrección de tu Hijo,
> a través de los signos sacramentales,
> que experimentemos siempre en nosotros
> un aumento de tu vida divina.
> Por Cristo, nuestro Señor.
> R. Amén.

RITO CONCLUSIVO

BENDICION

130. El sacerdote bendice a la persona enferma y a todos los presentes. Pero si ha quedado alguna partícula del Santísimo Sacramento, puede bendecir a la persona enferma haciendo la cruz con el relicario, en silencio.

Que nuestro Señor Jesucristo te acompañe y te defienda.
R. Amén.

Que te anteceda para guiarte, y vaya destrás de ti para protegerte.
R. Amén.

Que ponga sus ojos sobre ti, te guarde y te bendiga.
R. Amén.

Que te bendiga Dios todopoderoso,
Padre, Hijo + y Espíritu Santo.
R. Amén.

ANOINTING IN A HOSPITAL
OR INSTITUTION

INTRODUCTION

Have faith in God, and faith in me.

149 Although the sacrament of anointing should be celebrated whenever possible in accordance with the full rites already given, the special circumstances of hospital ministry often make it necessary to abbreviate the rite. The rite which follows is a simplification of the anointing rite and preserves its central elements. It is intended for those occasions when only the priest and sick person are present and the complete rite cannot be celebrated.

150 The priest should inquire beforehand about the physical and spiritual condition of the sick person in order to plan the celebration properly and choose the appropriate prayers. If possible he should involve the sick person in this preparation, and should explain the significance of the sacrament.

151 If the sick person wishes to celebrate the sacrament of penance, it is preferable that the priest make himself available for this during a previous visit. If it is necessary, this may take place during the introductory rites.

152 The circumstances of an emergency room or casualty ward of a hospital may make the proper celebration of the sacrament difficult. If the condition of the sick person does not make anointing urgent, the priest may find it better to wait for a more appropriate time to celebrate the sacrament.

153 The priest should arrange for the continued pastoral care of the sick person, especially for frequent opportunities to receive communion.

ANOINTING IN A HOSPITAL OR INSTITUTION

OUTLINE OF THE RITE

INTRODUCTORY RITES
Greeting
Instruction

LITURGY OF ANOINTING
Laying on of Hands
Anointing
Lord's Prayer
Prayer after Anointing

CONCLUDING RITE
Blessing

UNCION EN UN HOSPITAL U OTRA INSTITUCION

ESQUEMA DEL RITO

RITOS INTRODUCTORIOS
Saludo
Instrucción

LITURGIA DE LA UNCION
Imposición de las manos
Unción
Padrenuestro
Oración después de la unción

RITO CONCLUSIVO
Bendición

ANOINTING IN A HOSPITAL OR INSTITUTION

INTRODUCTORY RITES

GREETING

154 The priest greets the sick person.

The peace of the Lord be with you always.

R. And also with you.

INSTRUCTION

155 The priest may prepare the sick person for the liturgy of anointing with an instruction or with the following prayer:

Lord God,
you have said to us through your apostle James:
"Are there people sick among you?
Let them send for the priests of the Church,
and let the priests pray over them
anointing them with oil in the name of the Lord.
The prayer of faith will save the sick persons,
and the Lord will raise them up.
If they have committed any sins,
their sins will be forgiven them."

Lord,
we have gathered here in your name
and we ask you to be among us,
to watch over our brother/sister N.
We ask this with confidence,
for you live and reign for ever and ever.

R. Amen.

If the sick person so wishes, the sacrament of penance may now be celebrated.

UNCION EN UN HOSPITAL
U OTRA INSTITUCION

RITOS INTRODUCTORIOS

SALUDO

154. El sacerdote saluda al enfermo.

La paz del Señor esté siempre con ustedes.
R. Y también contigo.

INSTRUCCION

155. El sacerdote puede preparar a la persona enferma para la liturgia de la unción con una instrucción o con la siguiente oración:

Señor y Dios nuestro,
tú que nos enseñaste, por medio del apóstol Santiago:
"Hermanos: el que esté enfermo,
que llame a los presbíteros de la Iglesia
para que rueguen por él, ungiéndolo con aceite
en nombre del Señor.
La oración hecha con fe salvará al enfermo,
el Señor lo levantará y,
si ha cometido pecados, le serán perdonados" (Sant 5, 14-15)
te pedimos confiadamente que permanezcas entre nosotros,
que nos hemos congregado en tu nombre.

Protege con tu misericordia a nuestro(a) hermano(a) N.,
que se halla enfermo(a) (y a todos los demás enfermos
de esta casa).
Que vives y reinas por los siglos de los siglos.
R.   Amén.

Si la persona enferma lo desea, en este momento se le puede administrar el sacramento de la penitencia.

LITURGY OF ANOINTING

LAYING ON OF HANDS

156 In silence, the priest lays his hands on the head of the sick person.

ANOINTING

157 The priest anoints the sick person with the blessed oil.

First he anoints the forehead, saying:

**Through this holy anointing
may the Lord in his love and mercy help you
with the grace of the Holy Spirit.**

R. Amen.

Then he anoints the hands, saying:

**May the Lord who frees you from sin
save you and raise you up.**

R. Amen.

The sacramental form is said only once, for the anointing of the forehead and hands, and is not repeated.

Depending upon the culture and traditions of the place, as well as the condition of the sick person, the priest may also anoint additional parts of the body, for example, the area of pain or injury. He does not repeat the sacramental form.

LORD'S PRAYER

158 The priest introduces the Lord's Prayer in these or similar words:

Now let us pray to God as our Lord Jesus Christ taught us:

All say:

Our Father . . .

LITURGIA DE LA UNCION

156. El sacerdote le impone las manos a la persona enferma en la cabeza, en silencio.

UNCION

157. El sacerdote unge a la persona enferma con el aceite sagrado.

Primero le unge la frente, diciendo:

**POR ESTA SANTA UNCION
Y POR SU BONDADOSA MISERICORDIA
TE AYUDE EL SEÑOR CON LA GRACIA
DEL ESPIRITU SANTO.
R.   Amén.**

Después le unge las manos, diciendo:

**PARA QUE, LIBRE DE TUS PECADOS,
TE CONCEDA LA SALVACION
Y TE CONFORTE EN TU ENFERMEDAD.
R.   Amén.**

La forma sacramental se dice una sola vez para la unción de la frente y las manos, y no se repite.

De acuerdo con la cultura y tradiciones del lugar, y teniendo también en cuenta la condición de la persona enferma, el sacerdote puede ungir también algunas otras partes del cuerpo, por ejemplo, la región del dolor o de la herida. Pero lo hace sin repetir la fórmula de la unción.

PADRENUESTRO

158. El sacerdote introduce el padrenuestro con estas palabras u otras semejantes:

Oremos como Cristo nuestro Señor nos enseñó:

Todos dicen:

Padre nuestro. . .

PRAYER AFTER ANOINTING

159   The priest says the following prayer:

Father in heaven,
through this holy anointing
grant N. comfort in his/her suffering.

When he/she is afraid, give him/her courage,
when afflicted, give him/her patience,
when dejected, afford him/her hope,
and when alone, assure him/her of the support
    of your holy people.

We ask this through Christ our Lord.

R. Amen.

CONCLUDING RITE

BLESSING

160   Then the priest blesses the sick person.

May the blessing of almighty God,
the Father, and the Son, + and the Holy Spirit,
come upon you and remain with you for ever.

R. Amen.

ORACION DESPUES DE LA UNCION

159. El sacerdote dice la siguiente oración:

Padre nuestro del cielo,
por medio de esta unción
concede a nuesto(a) hermano(a)
el alivio de sus sufriimuentos
Cuando tenga ,iedo, concédele valor;
cuando se sienta afligido(a), dale paciencia;
cuando se sienta deprimido(a), concédele esperanza;
cuando se sienta solo(a),
dale la compañía de tu pueblo santo.
Te lo pedimos por Cristo, nuestro Señor.

R . Amén.

RITO CONCLUSIVO

BENDICION

160. A continuación el sacerdote bendice a la persona enferma, utilizando la siguiente fórmula:

La bendición de Dios todopoderoso,
Padre, Hijo + y Espíritu Santo,
descienda sobre ti (ustedes)
y permanezca para siempre.
R. Amén.

PART II

PASTORAL CARE OF THE DYING

Part II
PASTORAL CARE OF THE DYING

INTRODUCTION

When we were baptized in Christ Jesus we were baptized into his death . . . so that as Christ was raised from the dead by the Father's glory, we too might live a new life.

161 The rites in Part II of *Pastoral Care of the Sick: Rites of Anointing and Viaticum* are used by the Church to comfort and strengthen a dying Christian in the passage from this life. The ministry to the dying places emphasis on trust in the Lord's promise of eternal life rather than on the struggle against illness which is characteristic of the pastoral care of the sick.

The first three chapters of Part II provide for those situations in which time is not a pressing concern and the rites can be celebrated fully and properly. These are to be clearly distinguished from the rites contained in Chapter Eight, "Rites for Exceptional Circumstances," which provide for the emergency situations sometimes encountered in the ministry to the dying.

162 Priests with pastoral responsibilities are to direct the efforts of the family and friends as well as other ministers of the local Church in the care of the dying. They should ensure that all are familiar with the rites provided here.

The words "priest," "deacon," and "minister" are used advisedly. Only in those rites which must be celebrated by a priest is the word "priest" used in the rubrics (that is, the sacrament of penance, the sacrament of the anointing of the sick, the celebration of viaticum within Mass). Whenever it is clear that, in the absence of a priest, a deacon may preside at a particular rite, the words "priest or deacon" are used in the rubrics. Whenever another minister is permitted to celebrate a rite in the absence of a priest or deacon, the word "minister" is used in the rubrics, even though in many cases the rite will be celebrated by a priest or deacon.

163 The Christian community has a continuing responsibility to pray for and with the person who is dying. Through its sacramental ministry to the dying the community helps Christians to embrace death in mysterious union with the crucified and risen Lord, who awaits them in the fullness of life.

CELEBRATION OF VIATICUM

164 A rite for viaticum within Mass and another for viaticum outside Mass are provided. If possible, viaticum should take place within the full eucharistic celebration, with the family, friends, and other members of the Christian community taking part. The rite for viaticum outside Mass is used when the full eucharistic celebration cannot take place. Again, if it is possible, others should take part.

COMMENDATION OF THE DYING

165 The second chapter of Part II contains a collection of prayers for the spiritual comfort of the Christian who is close to death. These prayers are traditionally called the commendation of the dying to God and are to be used according to the circumstances of each case.

PRAYERS FOR THE DEAD

166 A chapter has also been provided to assist a minister who has been called to attend a person who is already dead. A priest is not to administer the sacrament of anointing. Instead, he should pray for the dead person, using prayers such as those which appear in this chapter. He may find it necessary to explain to the family of the person who is dead that sacraments are celebrated for the living, not for the dead, and that the dead are effectively helped by the prayers of the living.

RITES FOR EXCEPTIONAL CIRCUMSTANCES

167 Chapter Eight, "Rites for Exceptional Circumstances," contains rites which should be celebrated with a person who has suddenly been placed in proximate or immediate danger of death. They are for emergency circumstances and should be used only when such pressing conditions exist.

CARE OF A DYING CHILD

168 In its ministry to the dying the Church must also respond to the difficult circumstances of a dying child. Although no specific rites appear in Part II for the care of a dying child, these notes are provided to help bring into focus the various aspects of this ministry.

169 When parents learn that their child is dying, they are often bewildered and hurt. In their love for their son or daughter, they may be beset by temptations and doubts and find themselves asking: Why is God taking this child from us?

How have we sinned or failed that God would punish us in this way? Why is this innocent child being hurt?

Under these trying circumstances, much of the Church's ministry will be directed to the parents and family. While pain and suffering in an innocent child are difficult for others to bear, the Church helps the parents and family to accept what God has allowed to happen. It should be understood by all beforehand that this process of acceptance will probably extend beyond the death of the child. The concern of the Christian community should continue as long as necessary.

Concern for the child must be equal to that for the family. Those who deal with dying children observe that their faith matures rapidly. Though young children often seem to accept death more easily than adults, they will often experience a surprisingly mature anguish because of the pain which they see in their families.

170 At such a time, it is important for members of the Christian community to come to the support of the child and the family by prayer, visits, and other forms of assistance. Those who have lost children of their own have a ministry of consolation and support to the family. Hospital personnel (doctors, nurses, aides) should also be prepared to exercise a special role with the child as caring adults. Priests and deacons bear particular responsibility for overseeing all these elements of the Church's pastoral ministry. The minister should invite members of the community to use their individual gifts in this work of communal care and concern.

171 By conversation and brief services of readings and prayers, the minister may help the parents and family to see that their child is being called ahead of them to enter the kingdom and joy of the Lord. The period when the child is dying can become a special time of renewal and prayer for the family and close friends. The minister should help them to see that the child's sufferings are united to those of Jesus for the salvation of the whole world.

172 If it is appropriate, the priest should discuss with the parents the possibility of preparing and celebrating with the child the sacraments of initiation (baptism, confirmation, eucharist). The priest may baptize and confirm the child (see *Rite of Confirmation*, no. 7b). To complete the process of initiation, the child should also receive first communion.

According to the circumstances, some of these rites may be celebrated by a deacon or lay person. So that the child and family may receive full benefit from them, these rites are normally celebrated over a period of time. In this case, the minister should use the usual rites, that is, the *Rite of Baptism for Children*, the *Rite of Confirmation*, and if suitable, the *Rite of Penance*. Similarly, if time allows, the usual rites for anointing and viaticum should be celebrated.

173 If sudden illness or an accident has placed an uninitiated child in proximate danger of death, the minister uses "Christian Initiation for the Dying," adapting it for use with a child.

174 For an initiated child, or a child lacking only the sacrament of confirmation, who is in proximate danger of death, the "Continuous Rite of Penance, Anointing, and Viaticum" may be used and adapted to the understanding of the child. If death is imminent it should be remembered that viaticum rather than anointing is the sacrament for the dying.

Chapter Five

CELEBRATION OF VIATICUM

Chapter Five

CELEBRATION OF VIATICUM

INTRODUCTION

I am going to prepare a place for you; I shall come back and take you with me.

175 This chapter contains a rite for viaticum within Mass [not included in this edition] and a rite for viaticum outside Mass. The celebration of the eucharist as viaticum, food for the passage through death to eternal life, is the sacrament proper to the dying Christian. It is the completion and crown of the Christian life on this earth, signifying that the Christian follows the Lord to eternal glory and the banquet of the heavenly kingdom.

The sacrament of the anointing of the sick should be celebrated at the beginning of a serious illness. Viaticum, celebrated when death is close, will then be better understood as the last sacrament of Christian life.

176 Priests and other ministers entrusted with the spiritual care of the sick should do everything they can to ensure that those in proximate danger of death receive the body and blood of Christ as viaticum. At the earliest opportunity, the necessary preparation should be given to the dying person, family, and others who may take part.

177 Whenever it is possible, the dying Christian should be able to receive viaticum within Mass. In this way he or she shares fully, during the final moments of this life, in the eucharistic sacrifice, which proclaims the Lord's own passing through death to life. However, circumstances, such as confinement to a hospital ward or the very emergency which makes death imminent, may frequently make the complete eucharistic celebration impossible. In this case, the rite for viaticum outside Mass is appropriate. The minister should wear attire appropriate to this ministry.

178 Because the celebration of viaticum ordinarily takes place in the limited circumstances of the home, a hospital, or other institution, the simplifications

of the rite for Masses in small gatherings may be appropriate. Depending on the condition of the dying person, every effort should be made to involve him or her, the family, friends, and other members of the local community in the planning and celebration. Appropriate readings, prayers, and songs will help to foster the full participation of all. Because of this concern for participation, the minister should ensure that viaticum is celebrated while the dying person is still able to take part and respond.

179 A distinctive feature of the celebration of viaticum, whether within or outside Mass, is the renewal of the baptismal profession of faith by the dying person. This occurs after the homily and replaces the usual form of the profession of faith. Through the baptismal profession at the end of earthly life, the one who is dying uses the language of his or her initial commitment, which is renewed each Easter and on other occasions in the Christian life. In the context of viaticum, it is a renewal and fulfillment of initiation into the Christian mysteries, baptism leading to the eucharist.

180 The rites for viaticum within and outside Mass may include the sign of peace. The minister and all who are present embrace the dying Christian. In this and in other parts of the celebration the sense of leave-taking need not be concealed or denied, but the joy of Christian hope, which is the comfort and strength of the one near death, should also be evident.

181   As an indication that the reception of the eucharist by the dying Christian is a pledge of resurrection and food for the passage through death, the special words proper to viaticum are added: "May the Lord Jesus Christ protect you and lead you to eternal life." The dying person and all who are present may receive communion under both kinds. The sign of communion is more complete when received in this manner because it expresses more fully and clearly the nature of the eucharist as a meal, one which prepares all who take part in it for the heavenly banquet (see General Instruction of *The Roman Missal*, no. 240).

The minister should choose the manner of giving communion under both kinds which is suitable in the particular case. If the wine is consecrated at a Mass not celebrated in the presence of the sick person, the blood of the Lord is kept in a properly covered vessel and is placed in the tabernacle after communion. The precious blood should be carried to the sick person in a vessel which is closed in such a way as to eliminate all danger of spilling. If some of the precious blood remains after communion, it should be consumed by the minister, who should also see to it that the vessel is properly purified.

The sick who are unable to receive under the form of bread may receive under the form of wine alone. If the wine is consecrated at a Mass not celebrated in the presence of the sick person, the instructions given above are followed.

182 In addition to these elements of the rites which are to be given greater stress, special texts are provided for the general intercessions or litany and the final solemn blessing.

183 It often happens that a person who has received the eucharist as viaticum lingers in a grave condition or at the point of death for a period of days or longer. In these circumstances he or she should be given the opportunity to receive the eucharist as viaticum on successive days, frequently if not daily. This may take place during or outside Mass as particular conditions permit. The rite may be simplified according to the condition of the one who is dying.

VIATICUM OUTSIDE MASS

186 Although viaticum celebrated in the context of the full eucharistic celebration is always preferable, when it is not possible the rite for viaticum outside Mass is appropriate. This rite includes some of the elements of the Mass, especially a brief liturgy of the word. Depending on the circumstances and the condition of the dying person, this rite should also be a communal celebration. Every effort should be made to involve the dying person, family, friends, and members of the local community in the planning and celebration. The manner of celebration and the elements of the rite which are used should be accommodated to those present and the nearness of death.

187 If the dying person wishes to celebrate the sacrament of penance and this cannot take place during a previous visit, it should be celebrated before the rite of viaticum begins, especially if others are present. Alternatively, it may be celebrated during the rite of viaticum, replacing the penitential rite. At the discretion of the priest, the apostolic pardon may be added after the penitential rite or after the sacrament of penance.

188 An abbreviated liturgy of the word, ordinarily consisting of a single biblical reading, gives the minister an opportunity to explain the word of God in relation to viaticum. The sacrament should be described as the sacred food which strengthens the Christian for the passage through death to life in sure hope of the resurrection.

VIATICUM OUTSIDE MASS

OUTLINE OF THE RITE

INTRODUCTORY RITES

Greeting
Sprinkling with Holy Water
Instruction
Penitential Rite
[Apostolic Pardon]

LITURGY OF THE WORD

Reading
Homily
Baptismal Profession of Faith
Litany

LITURGY OF VIATICUM

Lord's Prayer
Communion as Viaticum
Silent Prayer
Prayer after Communion

CONCLUDING RITES

Blessing
Sign of Peace

EL VIATICO FUERA DE LA MISA

ESQUEMA DEL RITO

RITOS INTRODUCTORIOS
Saludo
Aspersión con agua bendita
Instrucción
Rito penitencial
Indulgencia plenaria en artículo de muerte

LITURGIA DE LA PALABRA
Lectura
Homilía
Profesión de fe bautismal
Letanías

LITURGIA DEL VIATICO
Padrenuestro
Comunión en forma de viático
Oración en silencio
Oración después de la comunión

RITOS CONCLUSIVOS
Bendición
Saludo de paz

VIATICUM OUTSIDE MASS

INTRODUCTORY RITES

GREETING

197 The minister greets the sick person and the others present.

The peace of the Lord be with you always.

R. And also with you.

The minister then places the blessed sacrament on the table, and all join in adoration.

SPRINKLING WITH HOLY WATER

198 If it seems desirable, the priest or deacon may sprinkle the sick person and those present with holy water.

Let this water call to mind our baptism into Christ,
who by his death and resurrection has redeemed us.

INSTRUCTION

199 Afterward the minister addresses those present, using the following instruction or one better suited to the sick person's condition.

My brothers and sisters, before our Lord Jesus Christ passed from this world to return to the Father, he left us the sacrament of his body and blood. When the hour comes for us to pass from this life and join him, he strengthens us with this food for our journey and comforts us by this pledge of our resurrection.

If the sacrament of penance is now celebrated the penitential rite is omitted. In case of necessity, this may be a generic confession.

VIATICO FUERA DE LA MISA

RITOS INTRODUCTORIOS

SALUDO

197. El ministro saluda a la persona enferma y a todos los presentes.

La paz del Señor esté siempre con ustedes.
R. Y también contigo.

El ministro coloca el Santísimo Sacramento en la mesa y todos lo adoran.

ASPERSION CON AGUA BENDITA

198. Si parece conveniente, el sacerdote o el diácono rocía con agua bendita a la persona enferma y a todos los presentes.

Que esta agua bendita nos recuerde
el bautismo que recibimos
y renueve nuestra fe en Cristo,
que con su muerte y resurrección nos redimió.

INSTRUCCION

199. Enseguida el ministro dirige a los presentes la siguiente instrucción u otra mejor, adaptada a la condición de la persona enferma.

Hermanos y hermanas: Antes de salir de este mundo hacia el Padre, nuestro Señor Jesucristo nos dejó el sacramento de su Cuerpo y de su Sangre. Y cuando a nosotros nos llegue la hora de pasar de esta vida para unirnos con él, él nos dará fuerza para el camino con este alimento y nos fortalecerá con la promesa de nuestra resurrección.

Si el sacramento de la penitencia se va a celebrar en este momento, se omite el rito penitencial. Y, si es necesario, basta con una confesión general.

PENITENTIAL RITE

200 The minister invites the sick person and all present to join in the penitential rite, using these or similar words:

My brothers and sisters, to prepare ourselves for this celebration, let us call to mind our sins.

After a brief period of silence, the penitential rite continues.

All say:

> I confess to almighty God,
> and to you, my brothers and sisters,
> that I have sinned through my own fault
>
>> They strike their breast.
>
> in my thoughts and in my words,
> in what I have done,
> and in what I have failed to do;
> and I ask blessed Mary, ever virgin,
> all the angels and saints,
> and you, my brothers and sisters,
> to pray for me to the Lord our God.

The minister concludes the penitential rite with the following:

May almighty God have mercy on us,
forgive us our sins,
and bring us to everlasting life.
R. Amen.

APOSTOLIC PARDON

201 At the conclusion of the sacrament of penance or the penitential rite, the priest may give the apostolic pardon for the dying.

Through the holy mysteries of our redemption,
may almighty God release you from all punishments
in this life and in the life to come.

May he open to you the gates of paradise
and welcome you to everlasting joy.

R. Amen.

RITO PENITENCIAL

200. El ministro invita a la persona enferma y a los presentes a unirse al rito penitencial, con las siguientes palabras:

Hermanos y hermanas, reconozcamos nuestros pecados
para disponernos a participar en esta celebración.

Después de un breve período de silencio, el rito penitencial prosigue.

Yo confieso ante Dios todopoderoso
y ante ustedes, hermanos,
que he pecado mucho,
de pensamiento, palabra, obra y omisión;
por mi culpa, por mi culpa, por mi gran culpa.

Se golpean el pecho.

Por eso ruego a santa María, siempre Virgen,
a los ángeles y a los santos
y a ustedes, hermanos,
que intercedan por mí ante Dios, nuestro Señor.

El ministro concluye el rito penitencial con las siguientes palabras:

Que Dios todopoderoso tenga misericordia de nosotros,
perdone nuestros pecados
y nos lleve a la vida eterna.
R. Amén.

INDULGENCIA PLENARIA EN ARTICULO DE MUERTE

201 Como conclusión del sacramento de la penitencia o del rito penitencial, el sacerdote puede conceder la indulgencia plenaria en artículo de muerte.

Por los santos misterios de nuestra redención,
Dios todopoderoso te perdone,
en esta vida y en la futura,
todas las penas que has merecido por tus pecados,
te abra las puertas del cielo
y te conduzca a la felicidad eterna.
R. Amén.

LITURGY OF THE WORD

READING

202 The word of God is proclaimed by one of those present or by the minister.

A reading from the holy gospel according to John   6:54-55

Jesus says:
"Anyone who does eat my flesh and drink my blood
has eternal life,
and I shall raise him up on the last day.
For my flesh is real food
and my blood is real drink."

This is the Gospel of the Lord.

HOMILY

203 Depending on circumstances, the minister may then give a brief
explanation of the reading.

BAPTISMAL PROFESSION OF FAITH

204 It is desirable that the sick person renew his or her baptismal profession of
faith before receiving viaticum. The minister gives a brief introduction and
then asks the following questions:

N., do you believe in God, the Father almighty,
creator of heaven and earth?

R. I do.

Do you believe in Jesus Christ, his only Son, our Lord,
who was born of the Virgin Mary,
was crucified, died, and was buried,
rose from the dead,
and is now seated at the right hand of the Father?

R. I do.

LITURGIA DE LA PALABRA

LECTURA

202. La palabra de Dios es proclamada por uno de los presentes o por el ministro.

Lectura del santo Evangelio según San Juan   6, 54-55

Jesús dice:
"El que come mi carne y bebe mi sangre,
vive de vida eterna, y yo lo resucitaré en el último día.
Mi carne es comida verdadera
y mi sangre es bebida verdadera."

Esta es palabra de Dios.

HOMILIA

203. De acuerdo con las circunstancias, el ministro puede hacer aquí una breve explicación de la lectura.

PROFESION DE FE BAUTISMAL

204. Es conveniente que la persona enferma renueve su fe bautismal, antes de recibir el viático. El ministro hace una breve introducción y después las siguientes preguntas:

N., ¿crees en Dios,
Padre todopoderoso,
creador del cielo y de la tierra?
R.   Sí creo.

¿Crees en Jesucristo,
su único Hijo, Señor nuestro,
que nació de la Virgen María,
padeció y murió por nosotros,
resucitó y está sentado a la derecha del Padre?
R.   Sí creo.

Do you believe in the Holy Spirit,
the holy catholic Church, the communion of saints,
the forgiveness of sins, the resurrection of the body,
and life everlasting?

R. I do.

LITANY

205 The minister may adapt or shorten the litany according to the condition of the sick person. The litany may be omitted if the sick person has made the profession of faith and appears to be tiring.

My brothers and sisters, with one heart let us call on our Savior Jesus Christ.

You loved us to the very end and gave yourself over to death in order to give us life. For our brother/sister, Lord, we pray:

R. Lord, hear our prayer.

You said to us: "All who eat my flesh and drink my blood will live for ever." For our brother/sister, Lord, we pray: R.

You invite us to join in the banquet where pain and sorrow, sadness and separation will be no more. For our brother/sister, Lord, we pray: R.

LITURGY OF VIATICUM

LORD'S PRAYER

206 The minister introduces the Lord's Prayer in these or similar words:

Now let us offer together the prayer our Lord Jesus Christ taught us:

All say:

Our Father . . .

¿Crees en el Espíritu Santo,
en la santa Iglesia católica, en la comunión de los santos,
en el perdón de los pecados, en la resurrección de los muertos
y en la vida eterna?
R.   Sí creo.

LETANIAS

205. El sacerdote puede adaptar (alargar, acortar) las letanías, de acuerdo con la condición de la persona enferma. Se pueden omitir las letanías, si la persona enferma ha hecho ya la profesión de fe y da señales de fatiga.

Hermanos y hermanas,
unámonos todos para invocar a nuestro Señor Jesucristo:

Señor nuestro, que nos amaste
hasta el extremo de entregarte a la muerte
para darnos la vida,
te rogamos por nuestro(a) hermano(a).
R .   Señor, escucha nuestra oración.

Señor nuestro, que dijiste:
"El que come mi carne y bebe mi sangre tiene la vida eterna",
te rogamos por nuestro(a) hermano(a).
R .   Señor, escucha nuestra oración.

Señor nuestro, que nos invitas a participar en tu Reino,
donde ya no hay dolor ni fatiga,
ni tristeza ni separación,
te rogamos por nuestro(a) hermano(a).
R .   Señor, escucha nuestra oración.

LITURGIA DEL VIATICO

PADRENUESTRO

206. El ministro introduce el padrenuestro con estas palabras u otras semejantes.

Digamos todos juntos la oración que nuestro Señor Jesucristo
nos enseñó:
Todos dicen:

Padre nuestro. . .

COMMUNION AS VIATICUM

207   The sick person and all present may receive communion under both kinds. When the minister gives communion to the sick person, the form for viaticum is used.

The minister shows the eucharistic bread to those present, saying:

Jesus Christ is the food for our journey;
he calls us to the heavenly table.

The sick person and all who are to receive communion say:

Lord, I am not worthy to receive you,
but only say the word and I shall be healed.

The minister goes to the sick person and, showing the blessed sacrament, says:

The body of Christ.

The sick person answers: "Amen."

Then the minister says:

The blood of Christ.

The sick person answers: "Amen."

Immediately, or after giving communion to the sick person, the minister adds:

May the Lord Jesus Christ protect you
and lead you to eternal life.

R. Amen.

Others present who wish to receive communion then do so in the usual way.

After the conclusion of the rite, the minister cleanses the vessel as usual.

SILENT PRAYER

208   Then a period of silence may be observed.

LA COMUNION COMO VIATICO

207. La persona enferma y todos los presentes pueden recibir la comunión bajo las dos especies. Pero cuando el ministro da la comunión a la persona enferma, utiliza la forma del viático.

El ministro muestra el pan eucarístico a todos los presentes, diciendo:

Jesucristo es el alimento para nuestro camino;
él nos llama a la mesa celestial.

La persona enferma y todos los que van a comulgar dicen:

Señor, yo no soy digno de que vengas a mí,
pero una palabra tuya bastará para sanarme.

El ministro se acerca a la persona enferma, y mostrándole el Santísimo Sacramento, le dice:

El Cuerpo de Cristo.

La persona enferma responde: "Amén".

Enseguida el ministro le dice:

La Sangre de Cristo.

La persona enferma responde: "Amén".

Inmediatamente después de darle la comunión a la persona enferma, el ministro añade:

Que el mismo Señor nuestro, Jesucristo,
te guarde y te lleve a la vida eterna.

La persona enferma responde: "Amén".

Las otras personas presentes que quieran comulgar lo hacen en la forma acostumbrada.

Concluido el rito, el ministro purifica los vasos sagrados como de ordinario.

ORACION EN SILENCIO

208. Después se puede guardar un período de silencio.

PRAYER AFTER COMMUNION

209   The minister says a concluding prayer.

Let us pray.

Pause for silent prayer, if this has not preceded.

God of peace,
you offer eternal healing to those who believe in you;
you have refreshed your servant N.
with food and drink from heaven:
lead him/her safely into the kingdom of light.

We ask this through Christ our Lord.

R. Amen.

CONCLUDING RITES

BLESSING

210   The priest or deacon blesses the sick person and the others present. If, however, any of the blessed sacrament remains, he may bless the sick person by making a sign of the cross with the blessed sacrament, in silence.

May the Lord be with you to protect you.
R. Amen.

May the Lord guide you and give you strength.
R. Amen.

May the Lord watch over you, keep you in his care,
and bless you with his peace.
R. Amen.

May almighty God bless you,
the Father, and the Son, + and the Holy Spirit.
R. Amen.

ORACION DESPUES DE LA COMUNION

209. El ministro dice una oración conclusiva.

Oremos.

Se guarda un momento de silencio para orar, si no se ha hecho con anterioridad.

Señor nuestro,
salvación eterna para los que creen en ti,
concede a nuestro(a) hermano(a) N.,
que, alimentado con el pan y el vino celestiales,
llegue con seguridad al Reino de la luz y de la vida.
Por Cristo, nuestro Señor.
R.   Amén.

RITOS CONCLUSIVOS

BENDICION

210. El sacerdote o el diácono bendice a la persona enferma y a todos los presentes. Sin embargo, si quedan algunos restos del Santísimo Sacramento, puede bendecir a la persona enferma haciendo, en silencio, una cruz con el Santísimo Sacramento.

Que nuestro Señor Jesucristo te acompañe y te defienda.
R.   Amén.
Que te anteceda para guiarte y vaya detrás de ti
para protegerte.
R.   Amén.
Que ponga sus ojos sobre ti, te guarde y te bendiga.
R.   Amén.

Que te bendiga Dios todopoderoso,
Padre, Hijo + y Espíritu Santo.
R.   Amén.

A minister who is not a priest or deacon invokes God's blessing and makes the sign of the cross on himself or herself, while saying:

May the Lord bless us,
protect us from all evil,
and bring us to everlasting life.

R.   Amen.

SIGN OF PEACE

211   The minister and the others present may then give the sick person the sign of peace.

Si el ministro no es ni sacerdote ni diácono, invoca la bendición de Dios y hace la señal de la cruz sobre sí mismo(a), mientras dice:

Que el Señor nos bendiga
nos libre de todo mal
y nos lleve a la vida eterna.
R.   Amén.

SALUDO DE PAZ

211. El ministro y las demás personas pueden dar a continuación el saludo de paz a la persona enferma.

Chapter Six

COMMENDATION OF THE DYING

Chapter Six

COMMENDATION OF THE DYING

INTRODUCTION

Into your hands, Lord, I commend my spirit.

212 In viaticum the dying person is united with Christ in his passage out of this world to the Father. Through the prayers for the commendation of the dying contained in this chapter, the Church helps to sustain this union until it is brought to fulfillment after death.

213 Christians have the responsibility of expressing their union in Christ by joining the dying person in prayer for God's mercy and for confidence in Christ. In particular, the presence of a priest or deacon shows more clearly that the Christian dies in the communion of the Church. He should assist the dying person and those present in the recitation of the prayers of commendation and, following death, he should lead those present in the prayer after death. If the priest or deacon is unable to be present because of other serious pastoral obligations, other members of the community should be prepared to assist with these prayers and should have the texts readily available to them.

214 The minister may choose texts from among the prayers, litanies, aspirations, psalms, and readings provided in this chapter, or others may be added. In the selection of these texts the minister should keep in mind the condition and piety of both the dying person and the members of the family who are present. The prayers are best said in a slow, quiet voice, alternating with periods of silence. If possible, the minister says one or more of the brief prayer formulas with the dying person. These may be softly repeated two or three times.

215 These texts are intended to help the dying person, if still conscious, to face the natural human anxiety about death by imitating Christ in his patient suffering and dying. The Christian will be helped to surmount his or her fear in the hope of heavenly life and resurrection through the power of Christ, who destroyed the power of death by his own dying.

Even if the dying person is not conscious, those who are present will draw consolation from these prayers and come to a better understanding of the paschal character of Christian death. This may be visibly expressed by making the sign of the cross on the forehead of the dying person, who was first signed with the cross at baptism.

216 Immediately after death has occurred, all may kneel while one of those present leads the prayers.

COMMENDATION OF THE DYING

CONTENTS OF THE CHAPTER

RECOMENDACION DEL ALMA

CONTENIDO DEL CAPITULO

Textos breves
Lectura
Letanías de los santos
Oración de recomendación del alma
Oración después de la muerte
Oración por la familia y amigos

COMMENDATION OF THE DYING

SHORT TEXTS

217 One or more of the following short texts may be recited with the dying person. If necessary, they may be softly repeated two or three times.

Who can separate us from the love of Christ?	Romans 8:35
Whether we live or die, we are the Lord's.	Romans 14:8
To you, Lord, I lift up my soul.	Psalm 25:1
The Lord is my light and my salvation.	Psalm 27:1
My soul thirsts for the living God.	Psalm 42:3

The Lord Jesus says,
I go to prepare a place for you,
and I will come again to take you to myself.   John 14:2-3

I desire that where I am,
they also may be with me,
says the Lord Jesus.   John 17:24

READING

218 The word of God is proclaimed by one of those present or by the minister. Selections from the following readings may be used:

Psalm 23

The Lord is my shepherd;
there is nothing I shall want.
Fresh and green are the pastures
where he gives me repose.
Near restful waters he leads me,
to revive my drooping spirit.

RECOMENDACION DEL ALMA

TEXTOS BREVES

217. Se pueden recitar uno o más de los textos siguientes con la persona moribunda. Si parece conveniente, se pueden repetir suavemente dos o tres veces.

"¿Quién nos separará del amor de Cristo?"   Rom. 8, 35

"Si vivimos, vivimos para el Señor, y si morimos,
morimos para el Señor".   Rom. 14, 8

"El Señor es mi luz y mi salud".   Salmo 27, 1

"Sediento estoy de Dios, del Dios que me da vida".   Salmo 42, 3

"Señor, mi Dios, a ti levanto mi alma. En ti confío".   Salmo 25, 1

"En la casa de mi Padre hay muchas mansiones", dice Jesús.   Jn. 14, 2

"Yo quiero que allí donde estoy yo, estén
también conmigo", dice Jesús.   Jn. 17, 24

LECTURA

218. Uno de los presentes o el ministro proclama la palabra de Dios. Para ello se pueden utilizar algunos trozos de los siguientes:

Salmo 23

El Señor es mi pastor, nada me falta,
en verdes pastos él me hace reposar
y adonde brota agua fresca me conduce.
Fortalece mi alma,
por el camino del bueno me dirige
por amor de su nombre.

He guides me along the right path;
he is true to his name.
If I should walk in the valley of darkness
no evil would I fear.
You are there with your crook and your staff;
with these you give me comfort.

You have prepared a banquet for me
in the sight of my foes.
My head you have anointed with oil;
my cup is overflowing.

Surely goodness and kindness shall follow me
all the days of my life.
In the Lord's own house shall I dwell
for ever and ever.

John 6:37-40

Jesus will raise his own from death and give them eternal life.

Jesus says:
"All that the Father gives me will come to me,
and whoever comes to me
I shall not turn him away;
because I have come from heaven,
not to do my own will,
but to do the will of the one who sent me.
Now the will of him who sent me
is that I should lose nothing
of all that he has given to me,
and that I should raise it up on the last day.

Yes, it is my Father's will
that whoever sees the Son and believes in him
shall have eternal life,
and that I shall raise him up on the last day."

Aunque pase por quebradas muy oscuras
no temo ningún mal,
porque tú estás conmigo,
tu bastón y tu vara me protegen.

Me sirves a la mesa
frente a mis adversarios,
con aceites tú perfumas mi cabeza
y rellenas mi copa.

Me acompaña tu bondad y tu favor
mientras dura mi vida,
mi mansión será la casa del Señor
por largo, largo tiempo.

Juan 6, 37-40

Jesús resucitará a los suyos de la muerte y les dará la vida eterna.

Jesús dice:
"Todo lo que el Padre me ha dado
vendrá a mí,
y yo no rechazaré al que venga a mí,
porque yo he bajado del cielo,
no para hacer mi propia voluntad,
sino la voluntad del que me ha enviado.
Y la voluntad del que me ha enviado
es que yo no pierda nada de lo que él me ha dado,
sino que lo resucite en el último día.
La voluntad de mi Padre es
que todo hombre que ve al Hijo y cree en él
tenga la vida eterna:
y yo lo resucitaré en el último día".

LITANY OF THE SAINTS

219 When the condition of the dying person calls for the use of brief forms of prayer, those who are present are encouraged to pray the litany of the saints — or at least some of its invocations — for him or her. Special mention may be made of the patron saints of the dying person, of the family, and of the parish. The litany may be said or sung in the usual way. Other customary prayers may also be used.

Lord, have mercy	Lord, have mercy
Christ, have mercy	Christ, have mercy
Lord, have mercy	Lord, have mercy
Holy Mary, Mother of God	pray for him/her
Holy angels of God	pray for him/her
Abraham, our father in faith	pray for him/her
David, leader of God's people	pray for him/her
All holy patriarchs and prophets	pray for him/her
Saint John the Baptist	pray for him/her
Saint Joseph	pray for him/her
Saint Peter and Saint Paul	pray for him/her
Saint Andrew	pray for him/her
Saint John	pray for him/her
Saint Mary Magdalene	pray for him/her
Saint Stephen	pray for him/her
Saint Ignatius	pray for him/her
Saint Lawrence	pray for him/her
Saint Perpetua and Saint Felicity	pray for him/her
Saint Agnes	pray for him/her
Saint Gregory	pray for him/her
Saint Augustine	pray for him/her
Saint Athanasius	pray for him/her
Saint Basil	pray for him/her
Saint Martin	pray for him/her
Saint Benedict	pray for him/her
Saint Francis and Saint Dominic	pray for him/her
Saint Francis Xavier	pray for him/her
Saint John Vianney	pray for him/her
Saint Catherine	pray for him/her
Saint Teresa	pray for him/her

LETANIAS DE LOS SANTOS

219. Cuando la condición de la persona enferma pide usar formas breves de oración, se recomienda a los presentes que recen las letanías de los santos —o por lo menos algunas invocaciones por el (la) enfermo(a). Especialmente se pueden mencionar los santos patronos: del (de la) moribundo(a), de la familia y de la parroquia. Las letanías se pueden recitar o cantar en la forma acostumbrada. Se pueden emplear, además, algunas otras oraciones conocidas.

Señor, ten piedad de nosotros	Señor, ten piedad de nosotros
Cristo, ten piedad de nosotros	Cristo, ten piedad de nosotros
Señor, ten piedad de nosotros	Señor, ten piedad de nosotros

Santa María, Madre de Dios	ruega por él (ella)
Santos ángeles de Dios	rueguen por él (ella)
Abraham, nuestro padre en la fe	ruega por él (ella)
David, jefe del pueblo de Dios	ruega por él (ella)
Todos los santos patriarcas y profetas	rueguen por él (ella)
San Juan Bautista	ruega por él (ella)
San José	ruega por él (ella)
San Pedro y san Pablo	rueguen por él (ella)
San Andrés	ruega por él (ella)
San Juan	ruega por él (ella)
Santa María Magdalena	ruega por él (ella)
San Esteban	ruega por él (ella)
San Ignacio de Antioquía	ruega por él (ella)
San Lorenzo	ruega por él (ella)
Santas Perpetua y Felícitas	rueguen por él (ella)
Santa Inés	ruega por él (ella)
San Gregorio	ruega por él (ella)
San Agustín	ruega por él (ella)
San Atanasio	ruega por él (ella)
San Basilio	ruega por él (ella)
San Martín	ruega por él (ella)
San Benito	ruega por él (ella)
San Francisco y Santo Domingo	rueguen por él (ella)
San Francisco Javier	ruega por él (ella)
San Juan María Vianney	ruega por él (ella)
Santa Catalina	ruega por él (ella)
Santa Teresa de Jesús	ruega por él (ella)

Other saints may be included here.

All holy men and women	pray for him/her

Lord, be merciful	Lord, save your people
From all evil	Lord, save your people
From every sin	Lord, save your people
From Satan's power	Lord, save your people
At the moment of death	Lord, save your people
From everlasting death	Lord, save your people
On the day of judgment	Lord, save your people
By your coming as man	Lord, save your people
By your suffering and cross	Lord, save your people
By your death and rising to new life	Lord, save your people
By your return in glory to the Father	Lord, save your people
By your gift of the Holy Spirit	Lord, save your people
By your coming again in glory	Lord, save your people

Be merciful to us sinners	Lord, hear our prayer
Bring N. to eternal life, first promised to him/her in baptism	Lord, hear our prayer
Raise N. on the last day, for he/she has eaten the bread of life	Lord, hear our prayer
Let N. share in your glory, for he/she has shared in your suffering and death	Lord, hear our prayer
Jesus, Son of the living God	Lord, hear our prayer

Christ, hear us	Christ, hear us
Lord Jesus, hear our prayer	Lord Jesus, hear our prayer

Aquí se pueden incluir otros santos.

Todos los santos, hombres y mujeres	rueguen por él (ella)

Señor, ten piedad	líbralo (a), Señor
De todo mal	líbralo (a), Señor
De todo pecado	líbralo (a), Señor
Del poder de Satanás	líbralo (a), Señor
En el momento de su muerte	líbralo (a), Señor
De la muerte eterna	líbralo (a), Señor
En el día del juicio	líbralo (a), Señor
Por tu encarnación	líbralo (a), Señor
Por tus sufrimientos y tu cruz	líbralo (a), Señor
Por tu muerte y resurrección	líbralo (a), Señor
Por tu retorno glorioso al Padre	líbralo (a), Señor
Por el don del Espíritu Santo	líbralo (a), Señor
Por tu nueva venida gloriosa	líbralo (a), Señor

Nosotros, que somos pecadores	te rogamos, óyenos
Conduce a N. a la vida eterna, que le prometiste en el bautismo	te rogamos, óyenos
Resucítalo (a) en el último día, pues él (ella) comió el pan de la vida	te rogamos, óyenos
Haz que N. comparta tu gloria, pues ha compartido tus sufrimientos y tu muerte	te rogamos, óyenos
Jesús, Hijo de Dios vivo	te rogamos, óyenos
Cristo, óyenos	Cristo, óyenos
Señor Jesús, escucha nuestra oración	Señor Jesús, escucha nuestra oración.

PRAYER OF COMMENDATION

220 When the moment of death seems near, some of the following prayers may
be said:

A Go forth, Christian soul, from this world
   in the name of God the almighty Father,
   who created you,
   in the name of Jesus Christ, Son of the living God,
   who suffered for you,
   in the name of the Holy Spirit,
   who was poured out upon you,
   go forth, faithful Christian.

   May you live in peace this day,
   may your home be with God in Zion,
   with Mary, the virgin Mother of God,
   with Joseph, and all the angels and saints.

B I commend you, my dear brother/sister,
     to almighty God,
   and entrust you to your Creator.
   May you return to him
   who formed you from the dust of the earth.
   May holy Mary, the angels, and all the saints
   come to meet you as you go forth from this life.
   May Christ who was crucified for you bring you
     freedom and peace.
   May Christ who died for you,
   admit you into his garden of paradise.
   May Christ, the true Shepherd,
   acknowledge you as one of his flock.
   May he forgive all your sins,
   and set you among those he has chosen.
   May you see your Redeemer face to face,
   and enjoy the vision of God for ever.

   ℟. Amen.

ORACION DE RECOMENDACION DEL ALMA

220. Cuando parezca cercano el momento de la muerte, se pueden rezar algunas de las siguientes oraciones.

A   Sal, alma cristiana, de este mundo,
en el nombre de Dios Padre todopoderoso, que te creó;
en el nombre de Jesucristo, Hijo de Dios vivo,
que padeció por ti;
en el nombre del Espíritu Santo, que te santificó.
Que descanses hoy en paz
y habites con Dios en su Reino,
en compañía de la Virgen Madre de Dios, María Santísima,
de san José y de todos los ángeles y santos.
R.   Amén.

B   Hermano (a) mío (a),
te pongo en manos de Dios todopoderoso,
para que vuelvas al mismo que te creó
y te formó del polvo de la tierra.
Cuando salgas de este mundo,
que vengan a tu encuentro la Santísima Virgen María,
los ángeles y todos los santos.
Nuestro Señor Jesucristo,
que quiso morir por ti en la cruz,
te libre de la muerte eterna.
El Hijo de Dios vivo te lleve a su Reino
y te reconozca entre sus ovejas, el buen pastor;
que él perdone tus pecados y te cuente entre sus elegidos;
que veas cara a cara a tu redentor
y goces de la contemplación de Dios
por los siglos de los siglos.
R.   Amén.

C Welcome your servant, Lord, into the place of salvation which because of your mercy he/she rightly hoped for.

R. Amen, or R.Lord, save your people.

Deliver your servant, Lord, from every distress.   R.

Deliver your servant, Lord, as you delivered Noah from the flood.   R.

Deliver your servant, Lord, as you delivered Abraham from Ur of the Chaldees.   R.

Deliver your servant, Lord, as you delivered Job from his sufferings.   R.

Deliver your servant, Lord, as you delivered Moses from the hand of the Pharaoh.   R.

Deliver your servant, Lord, as you delivered Daniel from the den of lions.   R.

Deliver your servant, Lord, as you delivered the three young men from the fiery furnace.   R.

Deliver your servant, Lord, as you delivered Susanna from her false accusers.   R.

Deliver your servant, Lord, as you delivered David from the attacks of Saul and Goliath.   R.

Deliver your servant, Lord, as you delivered Peter and Paul from prison.   R.

Deliver your servant, Lord, through Jesus our Savior, who suffered death for us and gave us eternal life.   R.

C   Dale, Señor, a tu hijo(a)
la eterna salvación que espera de tu misericordia.
R.   Amén.

Salva, Señor, a tu hijo(a)
de todas las tribulaciones.   R.

Salva, Señor, a tu hijo(a),
como salvaste a Noé del díluvio.   R.

Salva, Señor, a tu hijo(a),
como salvaste a Abraham de sus enemigos.   R.

Salva, Señor, a tu hijo(a),
como salvaste a Job de sus padecimientos.   R.

Salva, Señor, a tu hijo(a),
como salvaste a Moisés del poder del faraón.   R.

Salva, Señor, a tu hijo(a),
como salvaste a Daniel del foso de los leones.   R.

Salva, Señor, a tu hijo(a),
como salvaste a los tres jóvenes
del horno ardiente y del poder de un rey inicuo.   R.

Salva, Señor, a tu hijo(a),
como salvaste a Susana de la calumnia.   R.

Salva, Señor, a tu hijo(a),
como salvaste a David de las manos de Goliat
y de la persecución del rey Saúl.   R.

Salva, Señor, a tu hijo(a),
como salvaste a Pedro y a Pablo de la cárcel.   R.

Por Jesucristo, nuestro Salvador,
que padeció por nosotros una muerte tan amarga
y nos mereció la vida eterna,
salva, Señor, a este(a) hijo(a) tuyo(a).   R.

PRAYER AFTER DEATH

221   When death has occurred, one or more of the following prayers may be said:

A Saints of God, come to his/her aid!
   Come to meet him/her, angels of the Lord!

   R. Receive his/her soul and present him/her
       to God the Most High.

   May Christ, who called you, take you to himself;
   may angels lead you to Abraham's side.   R.

   The following prayer is added:

   Let us pray.

   All-powerful and merciful God,
   we commend to you N., your servant.
   In your mercy and love,
   blot out the sins he/she has committed
   through human weakness.
   In this world he/she has died:
   let him/her live with you for ever.

   We ask this through Christ our Lord.

   R. Amen.

B Psalm 130

   R. My soul hopes in the Lord.

   Out of the depths I cry to you, O Lord,
   Lord, hear my voice!
   O let your ears be attentive
   to the voice of my pleading.   R.

   My soul is waiting for the Lord,
   I count on his word.
   My soul is longing for the Lord
   more than watchman for daybreak.   R.

   Because with the Lord there is mercy
   and fullness of redemption,
   Israel indeed he will redeem
   from all its iniquity.   R.

ORACION DESPUES DE LA MUERTE

221. Después de la muerte se puede decir una o varias de las oraciones siguientes:

A   Vengan en su ayuda, santos de Dios;
salgan a su encuentro, ángeles del Señor.
R.   Reciban su alma y preséntenla ante el Altísimo.

Que te reciba Cristo, el mismo que te llamó;
y que el coro de los ángeles te introduzca en el cielo.
R.   Reciban su alma y preséntenla ante el Altísimo.

Y se añade la siguiente oración:

Oremos.
Te encomendamos, Señor, a tu hijo(a) N.,
a fin de que, muerto ya para el mundo, viva para ti.
Con tu infinita misericordia
perdona los pecados que la fragilidad humana
le haya hecho cometer.
Por Cristo, nuestro Señor.
R.   Amén.

B   Salmo 130

R.   Mi alma espera en el Señor.

Desde el abismo clamo a Ti, Señor,
escucha mi clamor,
que tus oídos pongan atención
a mi voz suplicante.   R.

Espero en el Señor,
mi alma espera y confía en su palabra,
mi alma aguarda al Señor
mucho más que a la aurora el centinela.   R.

Porque el Señor tiene misericordia
y hay en él abundante redención.
El Señor dejará libre a Israel
de todas sus maldades.   R.

The following prayer is added:

Let us pray.

God of love,
welcome into your presence
your son/daughter N., whom you have called
    from this life.
Release him/her from all his/her sins,
bless him/her with eternal light and peace,
raise him/her up to live for ever with all your saints
in the glory of the resurrection.
We ask this through Christ our Lord.

R. Amen.

C Psalm 23

R. Lord, remember me in your kingdom.

The Lord is my shepherd;
there is nothing I shall want.
Fresh and green are the pastures
where he gives me repose.
Near restful waters he leads me,
to revive my drooping spirit.

R. Lord, remember me in your kingdom.

He guides me along the right path;
he is true to his name.
If I should walk in the valley of darkness
no evil would I fear.
You are there with your crook and your staff;
with these you give me comfort.   R.

You have prepared a banquet for me
in the sight of my foes.
My head you have anointed with oil;
my cup is overflowing.   R.

Surely goodness and kindness shall follow me
all the days of my life.
In the Lord's own house shall I dwell
for ever and ever.   R.

Se añade la siguiente oración:

> Oremos.
> Señor nuestro, que eres amor,
> recibe en tu presencia
> a tu hijo(a) N., a quien has llamado de esta vida.
> Perdónale todos sus pecados,
> bendícelo(a) con tu luz y paz eternas,
> levántalo(a) para que viva para siempre con todos tus santos
> en la gloria de la resurrección.
> Te lo pedimos por Cristo, nuestro Señor.
>
> R . Amén.

C Salmo 23

R.   Señor, cuando estés en tu Reino, acuérdate de mí.

> El Señor es mi pastor, nada me falta,
> en verdes pastos él me hace reposar
> y a donde brota agua fresca me conduce.   R.
>
> Fortalece mi alma,
> por el camino del bueno me dirige
> por amor de su nombre.   R.
>
> Aunque pase por quebradas muy oscuras
> no temo ningún mal,
> porque tú estás conmigo,
> tu bastón y tu vara me protegen.   R.
>
> Me sirves a la mesa
> frente a mis adversarios,
> con aceites tú perfumas mi cabeza
> y rellenas mi copa.   R.
>
> Me acompaña tu bondad y tu favor
> mientras dura mi vida,
> mi mansión será la casa del Señor
> por largo, largo tiempo.   R.

The following prayer is added:

Let us pray.

God of mercy,
hear our prayers and be merciful
to your son/daughter N., whom you have called
    from this life.
Welcome him/her into the company of your saints,
in the kingdom of light and peace.

We ask this through Christ our Lord.

R. Amen.

PRAYER FOR THE FAMILY AND FRIENDS

222 The following prayer may be said:

Let us pray.

God of all consolation,
in your unending love and mercy for us
you turn the darkness of death
into the dawn of new life.
Show compassion to your people in their sorrow.

[Be our refuge and our strength
to lift us from the darkness of this grief
to the peace and light of your presence.]

Your Son, our Lord Jesus Christ,
by dying for us, conquered death
and by rising again, restored life.

May we then go forward eagerly to meet him,
and after our life on earth
be reunited with our brothers and sisters
where every tear will be wiped away.

We ask this through Christ our Lord.

R. Amen.

For the solace of those present the minister may conclude these prayers with a
simple blessing or with a symbolic gesture, for example, signing the forehead
with the sign of the cross. A priest or deacon may sprinkle the body with holy
water.

Y se dice la oración siguiente:

Oremos.
Señor Dios de misericordia,
escucha nuestras oraciones y compadécete
de tu hijo(a), a quien has llamado de esta vida.
Recíbelo(a), junto con todos tus santos
en tu Reino de luz y de paz.
Te lo pedimos por Cristo, nuestro Señor.
R. Amén.

ORACION POR LA FAMILIA Y LOS AMIGOS

222. Se puede decir la siguiente oración:

Oremos.

Señor de todo consuelo,
con tu interminable amor y misericordia por nosotros,
nos transformas la oscuridad de la muerte
en un amanecer de nueva vida.
Ten compasión de tu pueblo, que sufre.

(Sé tú, Señor, nuestro refugio y fortaleza;
levántanos de esta pena tan oscura
hacia la paz y la luz de tu presencia).

Nuestro Señor Jesucristo, tu Hijo,
al morir por nosotros, venció a la muerte,
y al resucitar, restauró la vida.

Haz, Señor, que caminemos siempre hacia adelante,
para que podamos encontrar a nuestro(a) hermano(a)
y después de nuestra vida aquí en la tierra,
volvamos a reunirnos con nuestros hermanos y hermanas,
en tu cielo, donde toda lágrima será enjugada.
Te lo pedimos por Cristo, nuestro Señor.
R. Amén.

Para descanso de los presentes, el ministro puede concluir estas oraciones con
una simple bendición o con un gesto simbólico, por ejemplo, haciendo la señal de la cruz en la frente del difunto. El sacerdote o el diácono pueden rociar
el cuerpo con agua bendita.

Chapter Seven

PRAYERS FOR THE DEAD

Chapter Seven

PRAYERS FOR THE DEAD

INTRODUCTION

I want those you have given me to be with me where I am.

223 This chapter contains prayers for use by a minister who has been called to attend a person who is already dead. A priest is not to administer the sacraments of penance or anointing. Instead, he should pray for the dead person using these or similar prayers.

224 It may be necessary to explain to the family of the person who is dead that sacraments are celebrated for the living, not for the dead, and that the dead are effectively helped by the prayers of the living.

225 To comfort those present the minister may conclude these prayers with a simple blessing or with a symbolic gesture, for example, making the sign of the cross on the forehead. A priest or deacon may sprinkle the body with holy water.

PRAYERS FOR THE DEAD

OUTLINE OF THE RITE

Greeting
Prayer
Reading
Litany
Lord's Prayer
Prayer of Commendation

ORACIONES POR LOS DIFUNTOS

ESQUEMA DEL RITO

Saludo
Oración
Lectura
Letanías
Padrenuestro
Oración conclusiva

PRAYERS FOR THE DEAD

GREETING

226 The minister greets those who are present, offering them sympathy and the consolation of faith, using the following or similar words:

In this moment of sorrow
the Lord is in our midst
and comforts us with his word:
Blessed are the sorrowful; they shall be consoled.

PRAYER

227 The minister then says one of the following prayers, commending the person who has just died to God's mercy and goodness:

Let us pray.

A Almighty and eternal God,
    hear our prayers for your son/daughter N.,
    whom you have called from this life to yourself.

   Grant him/her light, happiness, and peace.
   Let him/her pass in safety through the gates of death,
   and live for ever with all your saints
   in the light you promised to Abraham
   and to all his descendants in faith.

   Guard him/her from all harm
   and on that great day of resurrection and reward
   raise him/her up with all your saints.
   Pardon his/her sins
   and give him/her eternal life in your kingdom.

   We ask this through Christ our Lord.

   R. Amen.

ORACIONES POR LOS DIFUNTOS

SALUDO

226. El ministro saluda a los presentes, les demuestra su simpatía les ofrece el consuelo de la fe, utilizando la siguiente fórmula u otras parecidas.

Hermanos, en estos momentos de dolor
el Señor está con nosotros
y nos conforta con sus palabras:
"Felices los que lloran,
porque serán consolados".

ORACION

227. El sacerdote dice a continuación una de las siguientes oraciones para encomendar a la persona recién muerta a la misericordia y bondad de Dios.

Oremos.

A   Dios todopoderoso y eterno,
escucha nuestras oraciones en favor de tu hijo(a) N.,
a quien has llamado de esta vida a tu presencia.

Concédele gozar de la luz, la felicidad y la paz.
Hazlo(a) pasar con seguridad las puertas de la muerte
y vivir para siempre con todos tus santos,
iluminado(a) por la luz que prometiste a Abraham
y a todos sus descendientes en la fe.

Líbralo(a) de todo mal
y en el gran día de la resurrección y la recompensa,
resucítalo junto con todos tus santos.
Perdónale sus pecados
y concédele la vida eterna en tu Reino.
Te lo pedimos por Cristo, nuestro Señor.
R.   Amén.

B Loving and merciful God,
   we entrust our brother/sister to your mercy.

   You loved him/her greatly in this life:
   now that he/she is freed from all its cares,
   give him/her happiness and peace for ever.

   The old order has passed away:
   welcome him/her now into paradise
   where there will be no more sorrow,
   no more weeping or pain,
   but only peace and joy
   with Jesus, your Son,
   and the Holy Spirit
   for ever and ever.

   R. Amen.

READING

228 The word of God is proclaimed by one of those present or by the minister.
One of the following readings may be used:

A A reading from the holy gospel
   according to Luke   23:44-46

   It was now about the sixth hour and, with the sun eclipsed, a
   darkness came over the whole land until the ninth hour. The veil of
   the Temple was torn right down the middle; and when Jesus had
   cried out in a loud voice, he said, "Father, into your hands I commit
   my spirit." With these words he breathed his last.

   This is the Gospel of the Lord.

B A reading from the holy gospel
   according to John   11:3-7, 17, 20-27, 33-36, 41-45

   The sisters sent this message to Jesus, "Lord, the man you love is
   ill." On receiving the message, Jesus said, "This sickness will end
   not in death but in God's glory, and through it the Son of God will be
   glorified."

B   Dios de misericordia y de amor,
ponemos en tus manos amorosas a nuestro(a) hermano(a) N.
En esta vida tú le demostraste tu gran amor;
y ahora que ya está libre de toda preocupación,
concédele la felicidad y la paz eterna.

Su vida terrena ha terminado ya;
recíbelo(a) ahora en el paraíso,
en donde ya no habrá dolores,
ni lágrimas ni penas,
sino únicamente paz y alegría
con Jesús, tu Hijo,
y con el Espíritu Santo,
para siempre.
R.   Amén.

LECTURA

228. Uno de los presentes o el ministro proclaman la palabra de Dios. Se puede utilizar una lectura de las siguientes:

A   Lectura del santo Evangelio según San Lucas   23, 44-46

Como al mediodía, se ocultó el sol y todo el país quedó en tinieblas hasta las tres de la tarde. En ese momento la cortina del Templo se rasgó por la mitad, y Jesús gritó muy fuerte: "Padre, en tus manos encomiendo mi espíritu", y al decir estas palabras, expiró.
Esta es palabra de Dios.

B   Lectura del santo Evangelio según San Juan   11, 3-7, 17,
                                                                              20-27, 33-36, 41-45

Las dos hermanas mandaron decir a Jesús: "Señor, el que tú amas está enfermo". Jesús, al oírlo, declaró: "Esta enfermedad no es de muerte, sino para gloria de Dios, y por ella se manifestará la gloria del Hijo de Dios".

Jesus loved Martha and her sister and Lazarus, yet when he heard that Lazarus was ill he stayed where he was for two more days before saying to the disciples, "Let us go to Judaea."

On arriving, Jesus found that Lazarus had been in the tomb for four days already. When Martha heard that Jesus had come she went to meet him. Mary remained sitting in the house. Martha said to Jesus, "If you had been here, my brother would not have died, but I know that, even now, whatever you ask of God, he will grant you." "Your brother" said Jesus to her "will rise again." Martha said, "I know he will rise again at the resurrection on the last day." Jesus said:

> "I am the resurrection.
> If anyone believes in me, even though he dies
>   he will live,
> and whoever lives and believes in me
> will never die.
> Do you believe this?"

"Yes, Lord," she said "I believe that you are the Christ, the Son of God, the one who was to come into this world." At the sight of her tears, and those of the Jews who followed her, Jesus said in great distress, with a sigh that came straight from the heart, "Where have you put him?" They said, "Lord, come and see." Jesus wept; and the Jews said, "See how much he loved him!" Then Jesus lifted up his eyes and said:

> "Father, I thank you for hearing my prayer.
> I knew indeed that you always hear me,
> but I speak
> for the sake of all these who stand round me,
> so that they may believe it was you who sent me."

When he had said this, he cried in a loud voice, "Lazarus, here! Come out!" The dead man came out, his feet and hands bound with bands of stuff and a cloth round his face. Jesus said to them, "Unbind him, let him go free."

This is the Gospel of the Lord.

Jesús quería mucho a Marta, a su hermana y a Lázaro. Sin embargo, cuando se enteró de que Lázaro estaba enfermo, se quedó ahí dos días más. Despúes dijo a sus discípulos: "Volvamos a Judea".

Cuando llegó Jesús, Lázaro llevaba cuatro días en el sepulcro. Cuando Marta supo que Jesús venía en camino, salió a su encuentro, mientras que María permaneció en casa. Marta, pues, dijo a Jesús: "Si hubieras estado aquí, mi hermano no habría muerto. Pero cualquier cosa que pidas a Dios, yo sé que Dios te la dará".

Jesús dijo: "Tu hermano resucitará". Marta respondió: "Yo sé que resucitará en la resurrección de los muertos en el último día". Jesús dijo:

"Yo soy la Resurrección y la Vida.
El que cree en mí, aunque esté muerto, vivirá;
y el que haya creído en mí
no morirá para siempre.
¡Crees esto?"

Ella contestó: "Sí, Señor, yo siempre he creído que Tú eres el Cristo, el Hijo de Dios que ha de venir a este mundo". Al ver Jesús el llanto de María y de todos los judíos que estaban con ella, se conmovió hasta el alma. Preguntó: "¿Dónde lo enterraron?" Le contestaron: "Señor, ven a ver". Y Jesús lloró. Los judíos decían: "¡Miren cuánto lo quería!"

Jesús levantó los ojos al cielo y exclamó:
"Te doy gracias, Padre, porque has escuchado
    mi oración.
Yo sé que siempre me oyes.
Pero digo esto por la gente que está aquí,
para que crean que Tú me has enviado".

Al decir esto, gritó muy fuerte: "¡Lázaro, sal fuera!" Y salió el muerto. Tenía las manos y los pies vendados, y la cabeza cubierta con un velo, por lo que Jesús dijo: "Desátenlo y déjenlo caminar".

Esta es palabra de Dios.

LITANY

229 Then one of those present may lead the others in praying a brief form of the litany of the saints. (The full form of the litany of the saints may be found on p. 132.) Other saints may be added, including the patron saints of the dead person, of the family, and of the parish; saints to whom the deceased person may have had a special devotion may also be included.

Saints of God, come to his/her aid!
Come to meet him/her, angels of the Lord!

Holy Mary, Mother of God	pray for him/her
Saint Joseph	pray for him/her
Saint Peter and Saint Paul	pray for him/her

The following prayer is added:

God of mercy,
hear our prayers and be merciful
to your son/daughter N., whom you have called
    from this life.
Welcome him/her into the company of your saints,
in the kingdom of light and peace.

We ask this through Christ our Lord.

R. Amen.

LORD'S PRAYER

230 The minister introduces the Lord's Prayer in these or similar words:

With God there is mercy and fullness of redemption; let us pray as Jesus taught us to pray:

All say:

Our Father . . .

LETANIAS

229. Uno de los presentes puede ir guiando a los demás al rezar una breve forma de letanías a los santos. (La forma completa de estas letanías se encuentra en la p. 133.) Se pueden incluir otros santos, especialmente los santos patronos de la persona difunta, de la familia, de la parroquia y otros santos a quienes la persona difunta haya tenido devoción particular.

Santos de Dios, ¡vengan en su ayuda!
¡Salgan a encontrarlo(a), ángeles de Dios!

Santa María, Madre de Dios	ruega por él (ella)
San José	ruega por él (ella)
San Pedro y san Pablo	rueguen por él (ella)

Se puede añadir la siguiente oración:

Oremos.
Señor Dios de misericordia,
escucha nuestras oraciones y compadécete
de tu hijo(a), a quien has llamado de esta vida.
Recíbelo(a), junto con todos tus santos
en tu Reino de luz y de paz.
Te lo pedimos por Cristo, nuestro Señor.
R.   Amén.

PADRENUESTRO

230. El ministro introduce el padrenuestro con éstas u otras palabras semejantes:

Dios es infinitamente misericordioso para redimirnos;
oremos como Jesús nos enseñó:

Todos dicen:

Padre nuestro. . .

PRAYER OF COMMENDATION

231 The minister then concludes with the following prayer:

Lord Jesus, our Redeemer,
you willingly gave yourself up to death
so that all people might be saved
and pass from death into a new life.
Listen to our prayers,
look with love on your people
who mourn and pray for their brother/sister N.

Lord Jesus, holy and compassionate:
forgive N. his/her sins.
By dying you opened the gates of life
for those who believe in you:
do not let our brother/sister be parted from you,
but by your glorious power
give him/her light, joy, and peace in heaven
where you live for ever and ever.

R. Amen.

For the solace of those present the minister may conclude these prayers with a
simple blessing or with a symbolic gesture, for example, signing the forehead
with the sign of the cross. A priest or deacon may sprinkle the body with holy
water.

ORACION CONCLUSIVA

231. El ministro termina con la siguiente oración:

Señor Jesús, redentor nuestro,
tú te entregaste voluntariamente a la muerte
para que todos pudiéramos salvarnos
y pasar de la muerte a una vida nueva.
Escucha, Señor, nuestras oraciones
y mira con amor a tu pueblo,
que ora entristecido por la muerte de su hermano(a) N.

Señor Jesús, santo y compasivo:
perdónale sus pecados a nuestro(a) hermano(a) N.
Con tu muerte nos has abierto las puertas de la vida
a aquellos que creemos en ti.
No permitas que nuestro(a) hermano(a) se aparte de ti;
al contrario, con tu supremo poder
concédele gozar de la luz, la alegría y la paz en el cielo,
en donde vives tú para siempre.
R.   Amén.

Para descanso de los presentes, el ministro puede concluir estas oraciones con una simple bendición o con un gesto simbólico, por ejemplo, haciendo la señal de la cruz en la frente del difunto. El sacerdote o el diácono pueden rociar el cuerpo con agua bendita.

Chapter Eight

RITES FOR EXCEPTIONAL CIRCUMSTANCES

RITES FOR
EXCEPTIONAL CIRCUMSTANCES

INTRODUCTION

I am the gateway. Whoever enters through me will be safe.

232 The rites contained in this section are exclusively for use in exceptional circumstances. In all other cases, the more developed forms of pastoral care ought to be employed for the greater benefit of those members of the community who are dying and for the greater consolation of those who are close to them.

The exceptional circumstances for which these rites are provided arise when there is a genuine necessity, for example, when sudden illness or an accident or some other cause has placed one of the faithful in the proximate or immediate danger of death.

CONTINUOUS RITE

233 A "Continuous Rite of Penance, Anointing, and Viaticum" has been set out so that these sacraments may be given together in a single celebration. If the person is unable to receive holy communion, the priest can use this rite, omitting the liturgy of viaticum.

RITE FOR EMERGENCIES

234 If death seems imminent and there is not enough time to celebrate the three sacraments in the manner given in the continuous rite, the priest should proceed with the "Rite for Emergencies."

CONTINUOUS RITE OF PENANCE, ANOINTING, AND VIATICUM

INTRODUCTION

He will wipe away all tears from their eyes; there will be no more death, and no more mourning or sadness.

236 This rite has been provided for use when sudden illness, an accident, or some other cause has placed one of the faithful in danger of death. It makes possible the reception of the three sacraments of penance, anointing, and viaticum in a single celebration. It is not only for use at the point of death, but even possibly a day or so before when time or the condition of the dying person will not allow a more developed celebration of these sacraments over a period of time. In its pastoral ministry the Church always seeks to be as complete as possible, and with this continuous rite those who are in danger of death are prepared to face it sustained by all the spiritual means available to the Church.

237 The priest should be guided by the condition of the dying person in deciding how much of this rite should be celebrated and where it should be appropriately shortened or adapted. If the dying person wishes to celebrate the sacrament of penance, this should take place before the anointing and reception of communion as viaticum. If necessary, the dying person may confess at the beginning of the celebration, before the anointing. Otherwise, the penitential rite should be celebrated.

If the danger of death is imminent, the priest should anoint immediately with a single anointing and then give viaticum. If the circumstances are extreme, he should give viaticum immediately (see no. 30), without the anointing. The Rite for Emergencies has been designed for this situation. Christians in danger of death are bound by the precept of receiving communion so that in their passage from this life, they may be strengthened by the body of Christ, the pledge of the resurrection.

238 It is preferable not to celebrate the sacrament of confirmation and the sacrament of the anointing of the sick in a continuous rite. The two anointings can cause some confusion between the two sacraments. However, if the dying person has not been confirmed this sacrament may be celebrated immediately before the blessing of the oil of the sick. In this case, the imposition of hands which is part of the liturgy of anointing is omitted.

CONTINUOUS RITE OF PENANCE, ANOINTING, AND VIATICUM

OUTLINE OF THE RITE

INTRODUCTORY RITES
Greeting
Instruction

LITURGY OF PENANCE
Sacrament of Penance
[Penitential Rite]
[Apostolic Pardon]
Baptismal Profession of Faith
Litany

[LITURGY OF CONFIRMATION]

LITURGY OF ANOINTING
Laying on of Hands
Prayer over the Oil
Anointing
[Prayer after Anointing]

LITURGY OF VIATICUM
Lord's Prayer
Communion as Viaticum
Silent Prayer
Prayer after Communion

CONCLUDING RITES
Blessing
Sign of Peace

RITO CONTINUO DE
LA PENITENCIA, LA UNCION Y VIATICO

ESQUEMA DEL RITO

RITOS INTRODUCTORIOS
Saludo
Instrucción

LITURGIA PENITENCIAL
Sacramento de la penitencia
(Rito penitencial)
(Indulgencia plenaria en artículo de muerte)
Profesión de fe bautismal
Letanías

(LITURGIA DE LA CONFIRMACION)

LITURGIA DE LA UNCION
Imposición de las manos
Bendición del óleo
Unción
(Oración después de la unción)

LITURGIA DEL VIATICO
Padrenuestro
Comunión como viático
Oración en silencio
Oración después de la comunión

RITOS CONCLUSIVOS
Bendición
Saludo de paz

CONTINUOUS RITE OF PENANCE, ANOINTING, AND VIATICUM

INTRODUCTORY RITES

GREETING

239 The priest greets the sick person and the others present.

The peace of the Lord be with you always.

R. And also with you.

If viaticum is to take place during the rite, the priest then places the blessed sacrament on the table, and all join in adoration.

INSTRUCTION

240 If the occasion requires, the priest speaks to the sick person about the celebration of the sacraments.

Depending on the circumstances, he reads a brief gospel text or an instruction to invite the sick person to repentance and the love of God.

Matthew 11:28-30

Jesus says: "Come to me, all you who labor and are overburdened, and I will give you rest. Shoulder my yoke and learn from me, for I am gentle and humble in heart, and you will find rest for your souls. Yes, my yoke is easy and my burden light."

RITO CONTINUO DE LA
PENITENCIA, LA UNCION Y EL VIATICO

RITOS INTRODUCTORIOS

SALUDO

239. El sacerdote saluda a la persona enferma y a todos los presentes.

La paz del Señor esté siempre con ustedes.
R.   Y también contigo.

Si durante el rito se va a administrar el viático, el sacerdote coloca el Santísimo Sacramento en la mesa y todos lo adoran.

INSTRUCCION

240. Si hace falta, el sacerdote le explica a la persona enferma lo que significon los sacramentos.

De acuerdo con las circunstancias, el sacerdote lee un breve texto del Evangelio o una instrucción que sirva para invitar a la persona enferma al arrepentimiento y al amor de Dios.

Lectura del santo Evangelio según San Mateo   11, 28-30

Jesús dice: "Vengan a mí los que se sienten cargados y agobiados, porque yo los aliviaré. Carguen con mi yugo y aprendan de mí que soy paciente de corazón y humilde, y sus almas encontrarán alivio. Pues mi yugo es bueno y mi carga liviana".

LITURGY OF PENANCE

SACRAMENT OF PENANCE

241 If the sick person so wishes, the sacrament of penance is celebrated; in case of necessity, the confession may be generic.

The priest extends his hands over the penitent's head (or at least extends his right hand) and says:

God, the Father of mercies,
through the death and resurrection of his Son
has reconciled the world to himself
and sent the Holy Spirit among us
for the forgiveness of sins;
through the ministry of the Church
may God give you pardon and peace,
and **I absolve you from your sins**
in the name of the Father, and of the Son, ✝
and of the Holy Spirit.

R. Amen.

PENITENTIAL RITE

242 If there is no celebration of the sacrament of penance, the penitential rite takes place as usual. The priest invites the sick person and all present to join in the penitential rite using these or similar words:

My brothers and sisters, let us turn with confidence to the Lord and ask his forgiveness for all our sins.

After a brief period of silence, the penitential rite continues, using one of the following:

LITURGIA PENITENCIAL

SACRAMENTO DE LA PENITENCIA

241. Si la persona enferma lo desea, puede recibir el sacramento de la penitencia; y en caso de necesidad, su confesión puede ser general.

El sacerdote extiende las manos sobre la cabeza del penitente (o por lo menos su mano derecha) y dice:

Dios, Padre misericordioso,
que reconcilió al mundo consigo
por la muerte y la resurrección de su Hijo,
y envió al Espíritu Santo para el perdón de los pecados,
te conceda, por el ministerio de la Iglesia,
el perdón y la paz.

> Y YO TE ABSUELVO DE TUS PECADOS,
> EN EL NOMBRE DEL PADRE, Y DEL HIJO,
> + Y DEL ESPIRITU SANTO.
> R.   Amén.

RITO PENITENCIAL

242. Si no hay celebración del sacramento de la penitencia, entonces se realiza el rito penitencial, como de costumbre. El sacerdote invita a la persona enferma y a todos los presentes a unirse en el rito penitencial, con éstas u otras palabras parecidas:

Hermanos y hermanas, pongamos toda nuestra confianza en el Señor y pidámosle perdón por todos nuestros pecados.

Después de un breve período de silencio, el rito penitencial prosigue, con la siguiente fórmula:

All say:

I confess to almightly God,
and to you, my brothers and sisters,
that I have sinned through my own fault

They strike their breast.

in my thoughts and in my words,
in what I have done,
and in what I have failed to do;
and I ask blessed Mary, ever virgin,
all the angels and saints,
and you, my brothers and sisters,
to pray for me to the Lord our God.

The priest concludes the penitential rite with the following:

May almighty God have mercy on us,
forgive us our sins,
and bring us to everlasting life.

R. Amen.

APOSTOLIC PARDON

243 At the conclusion of the sacrament of penance or the penitential rite, the priest may give the apostolic pardon for the dying, using the following:

Through the holy mysteries of our redemption,
may almighty God release you from all punishments
in this life and in the life to come.

May he open to you the gates of paradise
and welcome you to everlasting joy.

R. Amen.

Todos dicen:

> Yo confieso ante Dios todopoderoso
> y ante ustedes, hermanos,
> que he pecado mucho,
> de pensamiento, palabra, obra y omisión;
> por mi culpa, por mi culpa, por mi gran culpa.

Se golpean el pecho.

> Por eso ruego a santa María, siempre Virgen,
> a los ángeles, a los santos
> y a ustedes, hermanos,
> que intercedan por mí ante Dios, nuestro Señor.

El sacerdote concluye el rito penitencial con las siguientes palabras:

Que Dios todopoderoso tenga misericordia de nosotros,
perdone nuestros pecados
y nos lleve a la vida eterna.
R.   Amén.

INDULGENCIA PLENARIA EN ARTICULO DE MUERTE

243. Como conclusión del sacramento de la penitencia o del rito penitencial, el sacerdote puede conceder la indulgencia plenaria en artículo de muerte, utilizando la sigiente fórmula:

> Por los santos misterios de nuestra redención,
> Dios todopoderoso te perdone,
> en esta vida y en la futura,
> todas las penas que has merecido por tus pecados,
> te abra las puertas del cielo
> y te conduzca a la felicidad eterna.
> R.   Amén.

BAPTISMAL PROFESSION OF FAITH

244 If the condition of the sick person permits, the baptismal profession of faith follows. The priest gives a brief introduction and then asks the following questions:

N., do you believe in God, the Father almighty,
creator of heaven and earth?

R. I do.

Do you believe in Jesus Christ, his only Son, our Lord,
who was born of the Virgin Mary,
was crucified, died, and was buried,
rose from the dead,
and is now seated at the right hand of the Father?

R. I do.

Do you believe in the Holy Spirit,
the holy catholic Church, the communion of saints,
the forgiveness of sins, the resurrection of the body,
and life everlasting?

R. I do.

The priest may sprinkle the sick person with holy water after the renewal of the baptismal profession of faith.

LITANY

245 The litany may be adapted to express the intentions of the sick person and of those present. The sick person, if able, and all present respond. The following may be used:

You bore our weakness and carried our sorrows:
Lord, have mercy.

R. Lord, have mercy.

You felt compassion for the crowd,
and went about doing good and healing the sick:
Christ, have mercy.

R. Christ, have mercy.

PROFESION DE FE BAUTISMAL

244. Si la condición de la persona enferma lo permite, se hace la profesión de fe bautismal. El sacerdote hace una breve introducción y después las siguientes preguntas:

N., ¿crees en Dios,
Padre todopoderoso,
creador del cielo y de la tierra?
R.   Sí creo.

¿Crees en Jesucristo,
su único Hijo, Señor nuestro,
que nació de la Virgen María,
padeció y murió por nosotros,
resucitó y está sentado a la derecha del Padre?
R.   Sí creo.

¿Crees en el Espíritu Santo,
en la santa Iglesia católica,
en la comunión de los santos,
en el perdón de los pecados,
en la resurrección de los muertos
y en la vida eterna?
R.   Sí creo.

El sacerdote puede rociar a la persona enferma con agua bendita, después de la profesión de fe bautismal.

LETANIAS

245. Las letanías se pueden adaptar, de modo que expresen las intenciones de la persona enferma y de los presentes. Si es posible, la persona enferma responde junto con los presentes. Se puede utilizar la siguiente fórmula:

Señor, tú, que tomaste sobre ti mismo
nuestras enfermedades,
y sufriste nuestras aflicciones:
Señor, ten piedad de nosotros.
R.   Señor, ten piedad de nosotros.

Tú, que te compadeciste de las multitudes
y pasaste por el mundo haciendo el bien
y sanando a los enfermos:
Cristo, ten piedad de nosotros.
R .   Cristo, ten piedad de nosotros.

You commanded your apostles
to lay their hands on the sick in your name:
Lord, have mercy.
R. Lord, have mercy.

LITURGY OF CONFIRMATION

246 It is highly appropriate that the initiation of every baptized Christian be completed by the sacraments of confirmation and the eucharist. If the sacrament of confirmation is celebrated in the same rite, the priest continues as indicated in "Christian Initiation for the Dying." In such a case, the laying on of hands which belongs to the anointing of the sick (see no. 247) is omitted.

LITURGY OF ANOINTING

LAYING ON OF HANDS

247 In silence, the priest then lays his hands on the head of the sick person.

PRAYER OVER THE OIL

248 In some situations the priest may bless the oil himself (see no. 21). Otherwise, he says a prayer of thanksgiving over oil already blessed.

THANKSGIVING OVER BLESSED OIL—If the oil is already blessed, the priest says the following prayer of thanksgiving over it:

Praise to you, God, the almighty Father.
You sent your Son to live among us
and bring us salvation.

R. Blessed be God who heals us in Christ.

Praise to you, God, the only-begotten Son.
You humbled yourself to share in our humanity,
and you heal our infirmities. R.

Tú, que mandaste a tus apóstoles
que impusieran las manos sobre los enfermos:
Señor, ten piedad de nosotros.
R.   Señor, ten piedad de nosotros.

LITURGIA DE LA CONFIRMACION

246. Es muy apropiado que la iniciación de todo cristiano bautizado se complete con
los sacramentos de la Confirmación y la Eucaristía. Si el sacramento de la confirma
ción se celebra en este mismo rito, el sacerdote prosigue como en la "Iniciación
Cristiana de los Moribundos". Y en este caso, la imposición de manos que acompaña a
la unción de los enfermos se omite (ver n. 247).

LITURGIA DE LA UNCION

IMPOSICION DE LAS MANOS

247. En silencio, el sacerdote impone las manos sobre la cabeza de la persona
enferma.

ORACION POR EL OLEO

248. En algunas ocasiones el mismo sacerdote puede bendecir el óleo (ver el
n. 21). Si no lo bendice, entonces recita una oración de acción de gracias por
el óleo ya bendecido.

Acción de gracias por el óleo ya bendecido. Si el aceite ha sido anteriormente
bendecido, el sacerdote dice la siguiente oración de acción de gracias:

Bendito seas, Dios Padre omnipotente,
que enviaste a tu hijo al mundo,
por nosotros y por nuestra salvación.
R.   Bendito seas por siempre, Señor.

Bendito seas, Dios Hijo unigénito,
que, haciéndote hombre como nosotros,
quisiste aliviar nuestras enfermedades.
R.   Bendito seas por siempre, Señor.

Praise to you, God, the Holy Spirit, the Consoler.
Your unfailing power gives us strength
in our bodily weakness. R.

God of mercy,
ease the sufferings and comfort the weakness
    of your servant N.
whom the Church anoints with this holy oil.

We ask this through Christ our Lord.

R. Amen.

BLESSING OF OIL—When the priest is to bless the oil during the rite, he uses the
following blessing:

Bless, + Lord, your gift of oil
and our brother/sister N.
that it may bring him/her relief.

ANOINTING

249 The priest anoints the sick person with the blessed oil.
First he anoints the forehead, saying:

**Through this holy anointing
may the Lord in his love and mercy help you
with the grace of the Holy Spirit.**

R. Amen.

Then he anoints the hands, saying:

**May the Lord who frees you from sin
save you and raise you up.**

R. Amen.

Bendito seas, Dios Espíritu Santo consolador,
que con tu ilimitado poder
sanas la debilidad de nuestro cuerpo.
R.   Bendito seas por siempre, Señor.

Muéstranos, Señor, tu bondad, y santifica con tu bendición
este óleo preparado para aliviar las dolencias de tus fieles,
a fin de que, cuantos sean ungidos con él,
se vean libres, mediante la oración de la fe,
de toda enfermedad.
Por Cristo, nuestro Señor.
R.   Amén.

Bendición del óleo.— Cuando el sacerdote bendice el óleo durante el rito, utiliza la siguiente bendición:

Señor, ben + dice este óleo, don tuyo,
y también a nuestro hermano(a) N.,
para que pueda servirle de alivio.

UNCION

249.   El sacerdote unge a la persona enferma con el aceite bendito.

Le unge primero la frente, diciendo:

**POR ESTA SANTA UNCION
Y POR SU BONDADOSA MISERICORDIA
TE AYUDE EL SEÑOR CON LA GRACIA
DEL ESPIRITU SANTO.**
R.   Amén.

Después le unge las manos, diciendo:

**PARA QUE, LIBRE DE TUS PECADOS,
TE CONCEDA LA SALVACION
Y TE CONFORTE EN TU ENFERMEDAD.**
R.   Amén.

The sacramental form is said only once, for the anointing of the forehead and hands, and is not repeated.

Depending upon the culture and traditions of the place, as well as the condition of the sick person, the priest may also anoint additional parts of the body, for example, the area of pain or injury. He does not repeat the sacramental form.

When viaticum is celebrated the following prayer is omitted.

PRAYER AFTER ANOINTING

250 The priest says the following prayer:

Lord Jesus Christ, Redeemer of the world,
you have shouldered the burden of our weakness
and borne our sufferings in your own passion and death.

Hear this prayer for our sick brother/sister N.
whom you have redeemed.
Strengthen his/her hope of salvation
and sustain him/her in body and soul,
for you live and reign for ever and ever.

R. Amen.

LITURGY OF VIATICUM

LORD'S PRAYER

251 The priest introduces the Lord's Prayer in these or similar words:

Jesus taught us to call God our Father, and so we have the courage to say:

All say:

Our Father . . .

La forma sacramental se dice una sola vez para la unción de la frente y las manos, y no se repite.

De acuerdo con la cultura y tradiciones del lugar, y teniendo también en cuenta la condición de la persona enferma, el sacerdote puede ungir también algunas otras partes del cuerpo, por ejemplo, la región del dolor o de la herida. Pero lo hace sin repetir la fórmula de la unción.

ORACION DESPUES DE LA UNCION

250.   El sacerdote dice la siguiente oración:

Señor nuestro, Jesucristo, redentor del mundo,
tú has querido cargar el peso de nuestra debilidad
y soportar nuestros sufrimientos en tu pasión y muerte.

Escucha la oración que te hacemos
por nuestro(a) hermano(a) enfermo(a) N.,
a quien tú has redimido.
Refuerza la esperanza que tiene de salvarse
y conforta su cuerpo y su alma,
tú, que vives y reinas por los siglos de los siglos.
R.   Amén.

LITURGIA DEL VIATICO

PADRENUESTRO

251.   El sacerdote introduce el padrenuestro con éstas u otras palabras semejantes:

Jesús nos enseñó a llamar "Padre" a Dios; por eso nosatrevemos a decir:

Todos dicen:

Padre nuestro. . .

COMMUNION AS VIATICUM

252   The sick person and all present may receive communion under both kinds. When the priest gives communion to the sick person, the form for viaticum is used.

The priest shows the eucharistic bread to those present, saying:

Jesus Christ is the food for our journey;
he calls us to the heavenly table.

The sick person and all who are to receive communion say:

Lord, I am not worthy to receive you,
but only say the word and I shall be healed.

The priest goes to the sick person and, showing the blessed sacrament, says:

The body of Christ.

The sick person answers: "Amen."

Then the priest says:

The blood of Christ.

The sick person answers: "Amen."

Immediately, or after giving communion to the sick person, the priest adds:

May the Lord Jesus Christ protect you
and lead you to eternal life.

R. Amen.

Others present who wish to receive communion then do so in the usual way.

After the conclusion of the rite, the priest cleanses the vessel as usual.

LA COMUNION COMO VIATICO

252. La persona enferma y todos los presentes pueden recibir la comunión bajo las dos especies. Cuando el sacerdote le da la comunión a la persona enferma, utiliza la fórmula del viático.

El sacerdote muestra el pan eucarístico a los presentes, diciendo:

Jesucristo es el alimento para nuestro camino;
él nos llama a la mesa celestial.

La persona enferma y todos los que van a comulgar dicen:

Señor, yo no soy digno de que vengas a mí,
pero una palabra tuya bastará para sanarme.

Entonces el sacerdote se dirige hacia la persona enferma, y mostrándole el Santísimo Sacramento, le dice:

El cuerpo de Cristo.

La persona enferma responde: Amén.

Enseguida el sacerdote le dice:

La Sangre de Cristo.

La persona enferma responde: Amén.

Inmediatamente después de darle la comunión a la persona enferma, el sacerdote añade:

Que el mismo Señor nuestro, Jesucristo,
te guarde y te lleve a la vida eterna.
R.   Amén.

Las demás personas que quieran comulgar lo hacen en la forma acostumbrada.

Terminado el rito, el sacerdote purifica los vasos sagrados, como de costumbre.

SILENT PRAYER

253 Then a period of silence may be observed.

PRAYER AFTER COMMUNION

254 The priest says a concluding prayer. The following may be used:

Let us pray.

Pause for silent prayer, if this has not preceded.

Father,
your Son, Jesus Christ, is our way, our truth,
    and our life.
Look with compassion on your servant N.
who has trusted in your promises.

You have refreshed him/her with the body
    and blood of your Son:
may he/she enter your kingdom in peace.

We ask this through Christ our Lord.

R. Amen.

CONCLUDING RITES

BLESSING

255 The priest blesses the sick person and the others present. If, however, any
of the blessed sacrament remains, he may bless the sick person by making a sign
of the cross with the blessed sacrament, in silence.

May the Lord be with you to protect you.
R. Amen.

May he guide you and give you strength.
R. Amen.

May he watch over you, keep you in his care,
and bless you with his peace.
R. Amen.

May almighty God bless you,
the Father, and the Son, + and the Holy Spirit.
R. Amen.

ORACION EN SILENCIO

253. A continuación se puede guardar un período de silencio.

ORACION DESPUES DE LA COMUNION

254. El sacerdote dice una oración conclusiva. Se puede utilizar la siguiente:

Oremos.

Pausa para orar en silencio, si no se ha hecho antes.

Dios nuestro, cuyo Hijo es para nosotros
el camino, la verdad y la vida,
mira con bondad a nuestro(a) hermano(a) N.,
que confía plenamente en tus promesas,
y haz que, fortalecido(a)
con el Cuerpo y la Sangre de tu Hijo,
llegue en paz a tu Reino.
Por Cristo, nuestro Señor.
R.   Amén.

RITOS CONCLUSIVOS

BENDICION

255. El sacerdote bendice a la persona enferma y a todos los presentes. Sin embargo, si quedó alguna partícula del Santísimo Sacramento, puede bendecir a la persona enferma haciendo, en silencio, la señal de la cruz con el Santísimo Sacramento.

Que nuestro Señor Jesucristo te acompañe y te defienda.
R.   Amén.

Que te anteceda para guiarte
y vaya detrás de ti para protegerte.
R.   Amén.

Que ponga sus ojos sobre ti, te guarde y te bendiga.
R.   Amén.

Que te bendiga Dios todopoderoso,
Padre, Hijo + y Espíritu Santo.
R.   Amén.

SIGN OF PEACE

256 The priest and the others present may then give the sick person the sign of peace.

257 If the person recovers somewhat, the priest or other minister may continue to give further pastoral care, bringing viaticum frequently, and using other prayers and blessings from the rite of visiting the sick.

258 When death has occurred, prayers may be offered for the dead person and for the family and friends. This may be done in any suitable place, including a hospital chapel or prayer room.

SEÑAL DE LA PAZ

256. El sacerdote y las demás personas presentes pueden darle al enfermo el saludo de paz.

257. Si la persona enferma se alivia considerablemente, el sacerdote u otro ministro puede seguirle dando los auxilios espirituales, llevándole el viático con frecuencia y recitando las oraciones y bendiciones tomadas del ritual para visitar a los enfermos.

258. Cuando sobreviene la muerte, se pueden hacer oraciones por la persona difunta, por su familia y sus amigos. Tales oraciones se pueden celebrar en cualquier sitio apropiado, por ejemplo, en la capilla de un hospital o en un oratorio.

RITE FOR EMERGENCIES

INTRODUCTION

I am at your side always.

259 There are extreme circumstances in which not even the continuous rite can be celebrated. These occur when the danger of death from injury or illness is sudden and unexpected or when the priest is not called to exercise his ministry until the person is at the point of death.

260 In such a situation of emergency the priest should offer every possible ministry of the Church as reverently and expeditiously as he can. He may be able to provide only the barest minimum of sacramental rites and forms of prayer, but even then he should add other appropriate prayers from the ritual to help the dying person and those who may be present.

261 If the dying person wishes, the sacrament of penance is celebrated first. If necessary, the confession may be generic. Because of the emergency situation, viaticum follows immediately. Christians in danger of death are bound by the precept to receive communion. If there is still sufficient time, the anointing of the sick may then be celebrated. The brief rite which follows has been provided for the celebration of these sacraments in such a situation. The priest should judge, in light of the particular circumstances, how much or how little of this rite is possible.

262 After the celebration of the abbreviated rite for emergencies, the priest should continue in prayer with the dying person, if possible, and with the family and friends, as suggested in the "Commendation of the Dying." When death has occurred, some of the prayers suggested at the end of the "Commendation of the Dying" may be said with the family and friends.

263 When a priest has been called to attend a person who is already dead, he is not to administer the sacrament of anointing. Instead, he should pray for the dead person, asking that God forgive his or her sins and graciously receive him or her into the kingdom. It is appropriate that he lead the family and friends, if they are present, in some of the prayers suggested at the end of the "Commendation of the Dying," as already mentioned. Sometimes the priest may find it necessary to explain to the family of the person who has died that sacraments

are celebrated for the living, not for the dead, and that the dead are effectively helped by the prayers of the living.

If the priest has reason to believe that the person is still living, he anoints him or her, saying the usual sacramental form.

RITE FOR EMERGENCIES

OUTLINE OF THE RITE

Sacrament of Penance
[Apostolic Pardon]

Lord's Prayer
Communion as Viaticum

[Prayer before Anointing]
Anointing

Concluding Prayer
Blessing
Sign of Peace

RITO PARA LAS EMERGENCIAS

ESQUEMA DEL RITO

Sacramento de la penitencia
(Indulgencia plenaria en artículo de muerte)

Padrenuestro
Comunión como viático

(Oración antes de la unción)
Unción

Oración conclusiva
Bendición
Saludo de paz

RITE FOR EMERGENCIES

SACRAMENT OF PENANCE

264 If the sick person so wishes, the sacrament of penance is celebrated; in case of necessity, the confession may be generic.

Then the priest extends his hands over the penitent's head (or at least extends his right hand) and says:

God, the Father of mercies,
through the death and resurrection of his Son
has reconciled the world to himself
and sent the Holy Spirit among us
for the forgiveness of sins;
through the ministry of the Church
may God give you pardon and peace,
and **I absolve you from your sins
in the name of the Father, and of the Son, +
and of the Holy Spirit.**

R. Amen.

APOSTOLIC PARDON

265 The priest may give the apostolic pardon for the dying:

Through the holy mysteries of our redemption,
may almighty God release you from all punishments
in this life and in the life to come.

May he open to you the gates of paradise
and welcome you to everlasting joy.

R. Amen.

RITUAL PARA LAS EMERGENCIAS

SACRAMENTO DE LA PENITENCIA

264. Si la persona enferma lo desea, puede recibir el sacramento de la penitencia; y en caso de necesidad, su confesión puede ser general.

El sacerdote extiende las manos sobre la cabeza del penitente (o por lo menos su mano derecha) y dice:

Dios, Padre misericordioso,
que reconcilió el mundo consigo
por la muerte y la resurrección de su Hijo,
y envió al Espíritu Santo para el perdón de los pecados,
te conceda, por el ministerio de la Iglesia,
el perdón y la paz.

**Y YO TE ABSUELVO DE TUS PECADOS,
EN EL NOMBRE DEL PADRE, Y DEL HIJO,
+ Y DEL ESPIRITU SANTO.
R. Amén.**

INDULGENCIA PLENARIA EN ARTICULO DE MUERTE

265. El sacerdote puede conceder esta indulgencia al moribundo.

Por los santos misterios de nuestra redención,
Dios todopoderoso te perdone,
en esta vida y en la futura,
todas las penas que has merecido por tus pecados,
te abra las puertas del cielo
y te conduzca a la felicidad eterna.
R. Amén.

LORD'S PRAYER

266 The priest introduces the Lord's Prayer:

Jesus taught us to call God our Father, and so we have the courage to say:

All say:

Our Father . . .

COMMUNION AS VIATICUM

267 The priest goes to the sick person and, showing the blessed sacrament, says:

The body of Christ.

The sick person answers: "Amen."

Then the priest says:

The blood of Christ.

The sick person answers: "Amen."

Immediately, or after giving communion to the sick person, the priest adds the form for viaticum:

May the Lord Jesus Christ protect you
and lead you to eternal life.

R. Amen.

Others present who wish to receive communion then do so in the usual way.

PRAYER BEFORE ANOINTING

268 The priest says:
Let us ask the Lord to come to our brother/sister N. with his merciful love, and grant him/her relief through this holy anointing. In faith we pray:

R. Lord, hear our prayer.

PADRENUESTRO

266. El sacerdote introduce así el padrenuestro:

Jesús nos enseñó llamar "Padre nuestro" a Dios, por eso nos atrevemos a decir:

Todos dicen:

Padre nuestro. . .

COMUNION COMO VIATICO

267. El sacerdote se acerca a la persona enferma, y mostrándole el Santísimo Sacramento, dice:

El Cuerpo de Cristo.

La persona enferma responde: "Amén".

Enseguida el sacerdote dice:

La Sangre de Cristo.

La persona enferma responde: "Amén".

Inmediatamente después de darle la comunión a la persona enferma, el sacerdote añade la fórmula del viático:

Que el mismo Señor nuestro, Jesucristo,
te guarde y te lleve a la vida eterna.
R.   Amén.

Las demás personas que quieran comulgar lo hacen en la forma acostumbrada.

ORACION ANTES DE LA UNCION

268. El sacerdote dice:

Pidamos al Señor que ayude con su amor misericordioso a nuestro(a) hermano(a) N. y que le conceda alivio mediante esta santa unción..Oremos con fe.
R.   Señor, escucha nuestra oración.

ANOINTING

269 The priest anoints the sick person with the blessed oil.

First he anoints the forehead, saying:

**Through this holy anointing
may the Lord in his love and mercy help you
with the grace of the Holy Spirit.**

R. Amen.

Then he anoints the hands, saying:

**May the Lord who frees you from sin
save you and raise you up.**

R. Amen.

The sacramental form is said only once, for the anointing of the forehead and hands, and is not repeated.

CONCLUDING PRAYER

270 The priest says the following prayer:

Father,
you readily take into account
every stirring of good will,
and you never refuse to pardon the sins
of those who seek your forgiveness.

Have mercy on your servant N.,
who has now entered the struggle of his/her final agony.
May this holy anointing and our prayer of faith
comfort and aid him/her in body and soul.
Forgive all his/her sins,
and protect him/her with your loving care.

UNCION

269. El sacerdote unge a la persona enferma con el aceite bendito.

Primero le unge la frente, diciendo:

**POR ESTA SANTA UNCION
Y POR SU BONDADOSA MISERICORDIA
TE AYUDE EL SEÑOR CON LA GRACIA
DEL ESPIRITU SANTO.
R. Amén.**

Después le unge las manos, diciendo:

**PARA QUE, LIBRE DE TUS PECADOS,
TE CONCEDA LA SALVACION
Y TE CONFORTE EN TU ENFERMEDAD.
R. Amén.**

La forma sacramental se dice una sola vez para la unción de la frente y las manos, y no se repite.

ORACION CONCLUSIVA

270. El sacerdote dice la siguiente oración:

Padre nuestro,
tú tomas en cuenta gustoso
toda manifestación de buena voluntad
y jamás te niegas a perdonar los pecados
de aquellos que buscan tu perdón.

Ten compasión de tu hijo(a) N.,
que acaba de entrar en la batalla de su agonía final.
Que esta santa unción y nuestra oración hecha con fe
lo(a) conforten y lo(a) ayuden en su cuerpo y en su alma.
Perdónale todos sus pecados
y protégelo(a) con tu tierno amor.

We ask this, Father, through your Son Jesus Christ,
because he has won the victory over death,
opened the way to eternal life,
and now lives and reigns with you for ever and ever.

R. Amen.

BLESSING

271 The priest blesses the sick person:

May the blessing of almighty God,
the Father, and the Son,' + and the Holy Spirit,
come upon you and remain with you for ever.

R. Amen.

SIGN OF PEACE

272 The priest and the others present may then give the sick person the sign of peace.

273 If the person recovers somewhat, the priest or other minister may continue to give further pastoral care, bringing viaticum frequently, and using other prayers and blessings from the rite of visiting the sick.

274 When death has occurred, prayers may be offered for the dead person and for the family and friends. This may be done in any suitable place, including a hospital chapel or prayer room.

Te lo pedimos, Padre, por tu Hijo, Jesucristo,
porque él ha triunfado de la muerte,
nos ha abierto el camino de la vida eterna
y ahora vive y reina contigo para siempre.
R. Amén.

BENDICION

271. El sacerdote bendice a la persona enferma:

La bendición de Dios todopoderoso,
Padre, Hijo + y Espíritu Santo,
descienda sobre ti y permanezca contigo para siempre.
R. Amén.

SEÑAL DE LA PAZ

272. El sacerdote y las demás personas presentes pueden darle al enfermo el saludo de paz.

273. Si la persona enferma se alivia considerablemente, el sacerdote u otro ministro puede seguirle dando los auxilios espirituales, llevándole el viático con frecuencia y recitando las oraciones y bendiciones tomadas del ritual para visitar a los enfermos.

274. Cuando sobreviene la muerte, se pueden hacer oraciones por la persona difunta, por su familia y sus amigos. Tales oraciones se pueden celebrar en cualquier sitio apropiado, por ejemplo, en la capilla de un hospital o en un oratorio.

Appendix

RITE FOR RECONCILIATION
OF INDIVIDUAL PENITENTS

OUTLINE OF THE RITE

RECEPTION OF THE PENITENT

Invitation to Trust
Revelation of State of Life

LITURGY OF RECONCILIATION

Confession of Sins
Acceptance of Satisfaction
Penitent's Prayer of Sorrow
Absolution

Apéndice

RITO PARA
LA RECONCILIACION INDIVIDUAL

ESQUEMA DEL RITO

RECEPCION DEL PENITENTE
Invitación a la confianza
Manifestación del estado de vida

LITURGIA DE LA RECONCILIACION
Confesión de los pecados
Aceptación de la satisfacción
Contrición del penitente
Absolución.

RITE FOR RECONCILIATION OF INDIVIDUAL PENITENTS

299 This form for celebrating the sacrament of penance is for use when it is necessary in the following cases: during communion of the sick; during the celebration of anointing; during the celebration of viaticum. As far as possible, the indications contained in the pastoral notes preceding these various rites should be observed.

RECEPTION OF THE PENITENT

INVITATION TO TRUST

300 Using the following or similar words, the priest invites the sick person to have trust in God:

May the grace of the Holy Spirit
fill your heart with light,
that you may confess your sins with loving trust
and come to know that God is merciful.

R. Amen.

REVELATION OF STATE OF LIFE

301 At this point, if the sick person is unknown to the priest, it is proper for the sick person to indicate his or her state in life, the time of the last confession, difficulties in leading the Christian life, and anything else which may help the priest to exercise his ministry.

RITO PARA

LA RECONCILIACION INDIVIDUAL

299.   Esta forma de administrar el sacramento de la penitencia se usa necesa-
riamente en los siguientes casos: en la comunión de los enfermos, en la celebración de la unción y en la administración del viático. En cuanto sea posible,
obsérvense las indicaciones contenidas en las notas pastorales, puestas al prin-
cipio del libro.

RECEPCION DEL PENITENTE

INVITACION A LA CONFIANZA

300.   Utilizando las siguientes palabras u otras similares, el sacerdote invita a la persona
enferma a poner su confianza en Dios:

Que la gracia del Espíritu Santo
ilumine tu corazón,
para que, lleno(a) de confianza, confieses tus pecados
y experimentes la misericordia de Dios.
R.   Amén.

MANIFESTACION DEL ESTADO DE VIDA

301.   Si en este punto la persona enferma es desconocida para el sacerdote, es
muy conveniente que la persona enferma le indique su estado de vida, cuándo
se confesó por última vez, sus dificultades para llevar una vida cristiana y todo
aquello que pueda ayudar al sacerdote a ejercer su ministerio.

LITURGY OF RECONCILIATION

CONFESSION OF SINS

302 Where it is the custom, the sick person may say a general formula for confession (for example, "I confess to Almighty God . . .") before confessing his or her sins.

The sick person then confesses his or her sins. If circumstances call for it, a generic confession is sufficient.

If necessary, the priest helps the person to make an integral confession and gives suitable counsel; he should make sure that such counsel is adapted to the circumstances.

The priest urges the sick person to sorrow for sins, underlining that through the sacrament of penance the Christian dies and rises with Christ and is thus renewed in the paschal mystery.

ACCEPTANCE OF SATISFACTION

303   Where it is opportune, the priest proposes an act of penance which the sick person accepts to make satisfaction for sin and to amend his or her life. The act of penance should serve not only to make up for the past, but also to help begin a new life and provide an antidote to weakness.

As far as possible, the penance should correspond to the seriousness and nature of the sins.

This act of penance may suitably take the form of prayer, self-denial, and especially the uniting of sufferings with those of Christ for the salvation of the world. This will underline the fact that sins and their forgiveness have a social aspect, and will emphasize the important role the sick have in praying with and for the rest of the community.

LITURGIA DE LA RECONCILIACION

CONFESION DE LOS PECADOS

302.   Donde se acostumbra, la persona enferma puede recitar la fórmula general de la confesión (por ejemplo: "Yo confieso, ante Dios todopoderoso...") antes de confesar sus pecados.

A continuación la persona enferma confiesa sus pecados. Si las circunstancias lo piden, basta con una confesión general.

Si es necesario, el sacerdote ayuda a la persona para que haga una confesión íntegra y le da consejos apropiados; pero debe tener cuidado de que sus consejos se adapten a las circunstancias.

El sacerdote estimula a la persona a que se arrepienta de sus pecados, haciendo resaltar que, mediante el sacramento de la penitencia, el cristiano muere y resucita con Cristo y por eso mismo es renovado en el misterio pascual.

ACEPTACION DE LA SATISFACCION

303.   Cuando parezca oportuno, el sacerdote propone una "penitencia" o "satisfacción", que la persona enferma acepta como una compensación por sus pecados y como una enmienda de su vida. Dicho acto de penitencia no ha de servir únicamente de satisfacción por lo pasado, sino también como una ayuda para comenzar una vida nueva y como un antídoto contra la debilidad.

En cuanto sea posible, el acto de penitencia debe guardar cierta relación con la gravedad y naturaleza de los pecados.

Conviene que este acto de penitencia sea una oración, un acto de generosidad y amor, y especialmente un acto de unión de los propios sufrimientos con los de Cristo, por la salvación del mundo. En esta forma se hace resaltar que los pecados y su perdón tienen un aspecto social y se enfatizará el importante papel que tienen las oraciones del enfermo que ora con la comunidad y para el bien de ella.

PENITENT'S PRAYER OF SORROW

304 The priest then asks the sick person to express his or her sorrow; this may be done using the following prayer or any other act of contrition which may be familiar to the penitent.

Lord Jesus,
you opened the eyes of the blind,
healed the sick,
forgave the sinful woman,
and after Peter's denial confirmed him in your love.
Listen to my prayer, forgive all my sins,
renew your love in my heart,
help me to live in perfect unity with my fellow Christians
that I may proclaim your saving power to all the world.

ABSOLUTION

305 Then the priest extends his hands over the head of the penitent (or at least extends his right hand); care should be taken that this gesture is not confused with the laying on of hands during anointing. He says:

God, the Father of mercies,
through the death and resurrection of his Son
has reconciled the world to himself
and sent the Holy Spirit among us
for the forgiveness of sins;
through the ministry of the Church
may God give you pardon and peace,
and **I absolve you from your sins**
in the name of the Father, and of the Son, ✛
and of the Holy Spirit.

R. Amen.

He concludes by saying:

The Lord has freed you from sin.
May he bring you safely to his kingdom in heaven.
Glory to him for ever.

R. Amen.

CONTRICION DEL PENITENTE

304. El sacerdote pide a la persona enferma que exprese su dolor (contrición). Para ello se puede utilizar la fórmula siguiente o cualquier otro acto de contrición que sepa el penitente.

Señor Jesús,
tú que hiciste que los ojos de los ciegos pudieran ver,
que sanaste a los enfermos,
que perdonaste a la mujer pecadora,
y que a Pedro, después de sus negaciones,
lo confirmaste en tu amor,
escucha mi oración y perdóname todos mis pecados,
haz que reviva tu amor en mi corazón,
ayúdame a vivir en perfecta caridad con mis hermanos,
para que así pueda proclamar ante todo el mundo
tu gracia salvadora.

ABSOLUCION

305. Entonces el sacerdote extiende sus manos sobre la cabeza del penitente (por lo menos su mano derecha). Conviene tener cuidado de que este ademán no se vaya a confundir con la imposición de manos de la unción. Y dice:

Dios, Padre misericordioso,
que reconcilió el mundo consigo
por la muerte y la resurrección de su Hijo,
y envió al Espíritu Santo para el perdón de los pecados,
te conceda, por el ministerio de la Iglesia,
el perdón y la paz.

**Y YO TE ABSUELVO DE TUS PECADOS,
EN EL NOMBRE DEL PADRE, Y DEL HIJO
+   Y DEL ESPIRITU SANTO.**
R.   Amén.

El sacerdote concluye con estas palabras:

El Señor te ha librado del pecado.
Que él te lleve sano y salvo hasta su reino celestial.
A él la gloria por los siglos de los siglos.
R.   Amén.